IMPLICATION FOR TOURISM PLANNING AND DESTINATION MANAGEMENT

By

David Carr

DISCOVERY PUBLISHING HOUSE PVT. LTD.
NEW DELHI-110 002

Published by:

DISCOVERY PUBLISHING HOUSE
4383/4B, Ansari Road, Darya Ganj
New Delhi-110 002 (India)
Phone : +91-11-23279245; 23253475; 43596065
Mobile: +91 9811179893 / +91 9871656464
E-mail : discoverybooksindia@gmail.com
orderdphbooks@gmail.com
namitwasan9@gmail.com
web : www.discoverypublishinggroup.com

First Published: **2011**

Reprinted: **2024**

ISBN: 978-81-8356-938-5

Implication for Tourism Planning and Destination Management

Printed at:
Infinity Imaging Systems
Delhi

Preface

Tourism marketing is defined in a number of ways. It could be defined as the "systematic and coordinated efforts exerted by the National Tourist Organisations and/or the - tourist enterprises at international, national and local levels to optimise the satisfaction of tourists, groups and individuals, in view of the sustained tourism growth."

The pro-poor tourism has to help the very poorest in developing countries has been receiving increasing attention by those involved in development and the issue has been addressed either through small scale projects in local communities and by Ministries of Tourism attempting to attract huge numbers of tourists. Research by the Overseas Development Institute suggests that neither is the best way to encourage tourists' money to reach the poorest as only 25% or less (far less in some cases) ever reaches the poor; successful examples of money reaching the poor include mountain climbing in Tanzania or cultural tourism in Luang Prabang, Laos.

The main role of retail travel agents is to provide to their customers a convenient location for the "purchase" of various elements of travel like transport, accommodation and several other ancillary services associated with holiday and travel. The travel agents act as booking agents for holidays and travel and disseminate information and give advice on such services.

The most important objective of a tourist enterprise is to achieve the best results. This to a larger extent depends on a properly conceived marketing plan through which a strategy is to be developed to achieve the best results. Through the segmentation process appropriate targets are identified and analysed. The marketing strategy thus developed would now attempt to penetrate and persuade the target markets through a variety of tools mainly promotion and advertising.

Planning is an integral part of tourism sector. Tourism planning in India was started in November, 1982 after tourism was recognized as an industry by the Planning Commission of India in June, 1982. Just after one decade in May, the National Action Plan for tourism was announced. The objectives of this landmark plan for tourism planning in India were: to enhance the economy category domestic tourism, to develop the tourist areas socially and economically, promote eco-friendly environment and the national heritage, to boost international tourism, to improve in world tourism India's share and to increase opportunities for employment in this sector. Where we stand today and what are the main hindrances in planning and its immediate implementation is all about this book will reveal to the readers.

—Author

Contents

CHAPTER–1

INTRODUCTION

Tourism is travel for recreational, leisure or business purposes. The World Tourism Organization defines tourists as people who "travel to and stay in places outside their usual environment for more than twenty-four hours and not more than one consecutive year for leisure, business and other purposes not related to the exercise of an activity remunerated from within the place visited."

Tourism has become a popular global leisure activity. In 2008, there were over 922 million international tourist arrivals, with a growth of 1.9% as compared to 2007. International tourism receipts grew to US$944 billion (euro 642 billion) in 2008, corresponding to an increase in real terms of 1.8%. As a result of the late-2000s recession, international travel demand suffered a strong slowdown beginning in June 2008, with growth in international tourism arrivals worldwide falling to 2% during the boreal summer months. This negative trend intensified during 2009, exacerbated in some countries due to the outbreak of the H1N1 influenza virus, resulting in a worldwide decline of 4% in 2009 to 880 million international tourists arrivals, and an estimated 6% decline in international tourism receipts.

Tourism is vital for many countries, such as Egypt, Greece, Lebanon, Spain, Malaysia and Thailand, and many island nations, such as The Bahamas, Fiji, Maldives,

Philippines and the Seychelles, due to the large intake of money for businesses with their goods and services and the opportunity for employment in the service industries associated with tourism. These service industries include transportation services, such as airlines, cruise ships and taxicabs, hospitality services, such as accommodations, including hotels and resorts, and entertainment venues, such as amusement parks, casinos, shopping malls, music venues and theatres.

Meaning of Tourism

According to AJ Burkart and S Medlik, "Tourism denotes the temporary short-term movement of people to destinations outside the place where they normally live and work and their activities during their stay at these destinations."

Douglas Foster opines, "Tourism is an activity involving a complex mixture of material and psychological elements. The material ones are accommodation, attractions and entertainment available. The psychological factors include a wide spectrum of attitudes and expectations." The ministry of Tourism, in its document, *National Ministry on Tourism* (Preface) created for the Government of India, states," Tourism is a composite industry. It consists of various segments, which can produce a wide range of products and services."

Travel involves physical transportation of people. Tourism, on the contrary, involves mental transportation of people. Tourism gives a new lease of life to the spirit of adventure and sustenance of a person. It takes him to new environments and places. The unique features of those new environments stimulate the mind of the person. He, in turn, starts looking at life from a new angle.

And that is because he had visited new (and unknown) tourist destinations. Some tourist spots make long lasting impressions on the mind of the person who travels to those spots. True, some others do not impress him. But the totality of experiences is able to create a unique effect in the mind of the tourist. This unique effect could last the lifetime of that tourist! Some people live only to cherish the memories of travel to foreign lands and their experiences during their tours. Thus, tourism is a great motivator and an ideal educator. It has been said that travel makes a man wiser and experienced. Tourism, on the other hand, makes him relaxed, spiritual and full of salvation of a unique kind.

Domestic Tourist

Similarly, a domestic tourist is one who travels more than fifty kilometres away from home and spends at least a night in a hotel, or some place where he has to pay. If a man goes to another city and stays with his uncle, he is not counted as a tourist. That is how we count domestic tourists in India. The definition of a domestic tourist varies from country to country. There is no standard definition acceptable to all countries, as in the case of international tourists. India limits the distance to fifty kilometres and the USA to hundred miles. Each State Tourism Department in India maintains a statistical cell to compile statistics on tourism.

In October, 1973, the Thirteenth General Assembly of the IUOTO was held at Caracas. It had recommended that a study be carried out at the global level to arrive at a standard definition of the term "domestic tourist."

In 1974-75, the IUOTO put forward the following definition :

"For statistical purpose, the term "domestic tourist" designates any person who travels within the country where he resides to a place other than his usual place of residence for at least twenty-four hours or one night, for a purpose other than exercising a gainful activity and which may be classified under one of the following headings :—

1. Leisure (recreation, holiday, health, study, religion and sport).
2. Business, family, mission and meeting.

But this definition was not adopted as an official one. It was taken as a basis for discussions. The definitions being used now-a-days have 3 common elements, as follows :—

(a) *Place of Residence :* Most of the nations consider domestic tourism as travel by the residents of the country within that country.

(b) *Geographical Setting :* The operators of domestic tourism activities consider the national territory of the country as the geographical setting.

(c) *Duration of Travel :* A domestic tourist is one who spends not less than twenty-four hours or makes an overnight stay away from his usual residence. The night spent at an accommodation establishment (like hotel, lodge etc.) is important in this context.

(d) *Distance Travelled :* Some countries have defined the minimum distance to be travelled by domestic tourists so that they could be put under the category (of domestic tourism). This distance varies between *25 miles (40 km)* and *100 miles (160 km).*

But in modern times, this norm could be different. For example, a tourist may have to travel hundreds of *kilometres* to move from the eastern coast of the USA to her western coast. As another example, we can quote the case of travel of a tourist from New Delhi to Kanyakumari. The distance between Kanyakumari and New Delhi is more than *3,000 km.* But still, the tourist in question remains a domestic one because he is a resident of New Delhi.

(e) *Travel Motivation :* A domestic tourist is a person who travels for a purpose other than exercising a gainful activity at the place visited by him. But many domestic tourists purchase goods from the places of their visit. They come back and sell those goods in the local markets that are close to their residential areas. So, a combination of fun and business cannot be ruled out even during domestic tourist campaigns. In most of such cases, however, domestic tourism is undertaken for spending holidays or undertaking activities involving leisure.

Forest Tourist

The recommendations of the UN Conference on International Travel and Tourism, held in Rome in 1963, paved the way for defining this vital term. Consequently, the Government of India's Department of Tourism adopted a definition of this term according to these recommendations. This definition is as follows:

"A foreign tourist is a person visiting India on a foreign passport, staying for at least twenty-four hours in India and the purpose of whose journey can be classified under one of the following headings :—

1. Leisure (recreation, holiday), health, studies, religion and sports.
2. Business, family, mission or meeting.

The following persons are not deemed foreign tourists in India :—

1. Persons arriving, with or without contracts, to take up an occupation or engage in activities remunerated from within the country.
2. Persons coming to set up their residential places in the country.
3. Same-day visitors, which means those visitors who stay for less than *24 hours* in the country and include cruise travellers.

Finally, the following categories of travellers are not included in the category of foreign tourism :—

1. Nationals of Nepal who enter India through land routes from the Indo-Nepalese border.

2. All foreigners entering India from Bhutan by land.
3. Children of age less than 3 years.

International Nature

The terms related to a foreign tourist have been clearly mentioned in this section. When a tourist crosses the boundaries of the nation of his residence/citizenship, he is called Foreign Tourist. There are some restrictions on this definition. Barring such restrictions, the person is deemed a foreign tourist. However, other nations may define different norms to define a "foreign tourist" as per the rules of the IUOTO, WTO or IATA. They follow the globally accepted rules in such cases. International tourism and foreign tourism are being taken as synonymous phrases. All the activities related to the movement, stay, leisure, excursion, business and health of foreign tourists fall under the gamut of the term International Tourism. Several organisations like the IUOTO, PATA, WTO, IOTO etc. have defined certain norms and rules for conducting activities related to international tourism. Nations become the members of such organisations and follow their norms or codes of conduct.

Over a period of time, a set of rules has evolved for conducting international tourist operations. All such rules (arid operations governed by such rules) fall under the gamut of international tourism. If a nation wishes to earn more foreign exchange and give a fillip to her business and economic growth rates, she had better concentrate on international tourism. This activity not only helps the nation in question earn valuable international (hard) currencies, but also it helps her build an image of human-friendly, politically suave and liberal nation at the global fora (like the UNO).

Modern Tourism

The concept of modern tourism, as we understand it today, is relatively new—not more than sixty years old. Our world has become small. Every place on our earth is now known and shown on the maps. No new America or India remain to be discovered. The barriers of distance have been broken in the last two centuries, by the invention of steamships, railways, motor cars and the latest in the line, aeroplanes. A man can now have breakfast in London, lunch in New York and dinner in Tokyo.

A lot of good things have happened to the human race. Industrialisation has made the life of man easy. He does not have to work as hard as he did a hundred years ago. He gets holidays from work—in some countries people work only four days in a week and the remaining three days are holidays. Some companies allow their employees to choose their working hours. Besides, there are paid holidays every year. Several companies encourage their employees to go for a holiday once in a year and subsidises their travel. The result is a travel boom all over the world.

It has been estimated that five thousand million people take holidays, worldwide, every year. Of these, six hundred and ninety-eight million travelled internationally or to foreign countries, in the year 2000—a growth of 7.4 per cent over 1999. International travellers spent US$476 billion on travel—a growth of 4.5 per cent over the previous year—recipts per arrival were US$700 (Statistics WTO-2001). World Tourism Organisation (WTO) also estimates that international tourist arrivals will exceed one thousand six hundred million by the year 2020.

This is called tourism—people travelling for pleasure or on business, staying in hotels and spending their hard-earned money at places where they do not normally reside or make a living. It is a new economic phenomenon, a new business, a new industry of vast dimensions and magnitude.

The expenditure incurred by such people in areas other than their own place of residence, brings about prosperity in the areas receiving the visitor, and creates new jobs for the local population. As a result of tourism, the people of the world are coming closer to each other. It must be remembered that tourism can flourish only if there is peace on earth. Any disturbance of peace hurts tourism, as we witnessed during the Gulf War in January 1991—it affected tourism all over the world. Or, America's war on Afghanistan in 2001. International travel was disrupted badly. And, India mobilising its forcces on Indo-Pak border in early 2002. The Tourism was the first casualty.

Various Types

Man

It is the most vital resource of an organisation, department, state or country. Human Resource Management (HRM) is studied because management thinkers opine that humans are the most vital resource of the organisation. Money can be created, machines can be rebuilt, land can be purchased again and technologies can be altered to suit the need of a firm. But once a set of humans (trained employees) leaves a firm, the latter cannot recover from this shock, which can have social, economic and market-specific implications. As we move up the hierarchy of a firm, the human resource becomes more important with each step we take towards the owner(s) of that firm.

Machine

This resource refers to the equipment, services, machines and other processing, inspection and testing gadgets that a firm uses to manufacture its products. All the products made by a firm ultimately give services to their users (customers). Good-quality products give good services and bad-quality products give bad ones. Despite the fact that machines depend upon technologies of various types, their use, purchase, overhaul and redundancy depend upon the market pries.

Money

True, it makes the mare go ! No firm or individuals can survive without it.

Material

These are the raw materials. Finished components, work-in-process goods, spare parts, accessories, oils and lubricants, toots, jigs and figures, office equipment and stationery and other similar things. These are used directly (so that they fully enter the final product), partially (so that they enter the final product only partially) or indirectly (sot that they do not enter the final product but are used to make it).

Organisation

This refers to the organisation structure that a firm/ organisation owns to achieve its objectives. This structure defines line-staff relations, flow of communication, channels of communication, various departments and authority levels.

Methods

These comprise the technologies of manufacturing, processing, purchasing, delivery and service. Procedures for executing tasks are also a part of such methods as help the organisation achieve its coveted objectives.

Tourism Product

Tourism product is a unique concept in the parlance of tourism that satisfies some specific needs of the customer (tourist). Six P's of marketing have been defined by Phillip Kotler. Out of these, the first P (Product) assumes importance because it is something that is actually delivered to the customer. Further, Kotler has also pointed out that every product gives a service of some kind. So, all the products, gadgets, equipment etc. deliver services; these are not meant to be kept in a showcase simply because these are attractive by virtue of their packaging and features, according to Kotler. There are 6 basic components of a tourism product.

Accommodation

In this component, graded hotels, non-graded hotels, heritage hotels, inns, *sarais, havelis* and drive-in hotels (motels on highways) are included. For the tourism industry, the buildings of such hotels, *sarais, havelis* etc. as well as the sundry facilities associated with these buildings are deemed resources. Such resources also include gardens, parks, clubs, swimming pools, huts, orchids and other attractive parts of these buildings or premises. Tourists use these places or spots for staying (for brief periods). They pay for staying in such hotels and motels. Thus, this resource helps the owners of hotels or motels earn money. Properties located at prime spots of a city or tourist spot naturally cost more. Hence, owners of these properties charge more from their clients in terms of accommodation fees. Taxes are levied in excess by the government for these spots. So, the tourist has to shell out more money in five-star and five-star deluxe hotels of New Delhi, Kolkata and Mumbai. Further, if the hotel or place of stay is located at a remote place, or if it is only one of its kind at that place, the tourist has to spend more money. That is because temporary places of stay demand more funds for their maintenance at such remotely located spots. Further, religious places, beaches, fun parks etc., also have such hotels or inns as are quite costly because of the attraction for these spots. Tourists do not mind spending extra to stay at such spots. Example : The hotels of Genting Highlands Resort (Malaysia).

Recreation

This component of the product comprises activities of night-life, musical programmes, dance shows, theatre shows, cultural programmes and many more to tourists. They enjoy the unique cultural and social activities and festivals because they have come from different parts of the world. In this context, the dance and drama troupes (humans), various types of equipment (like drums, electronic playing services), furniture (facilities) etc., are a part of resources. Humans (the dancers, local people, tribal groups etc.), who actually present these shows, are also the resources for a tourism organisation. Example : The night show at Alcazar (Pattaya).

Restaurant

It includes bars, food joints, food cafes, dining halls within hotels etc. Various types of foods are offered to guests. Continental, American, Chinese, Indian and European cuisine are available in many hotels and restaurants. Guests choose according to their tastes and eating habits. But they may break away from their traditional food habits and try new cuisine too. Religion plays an important part in this context, however. The Hindus do not consume beef and the Muslims shun pork, to quote an example. All the food items and equipment used to process these and finished products brought from outside (to be served as such to guests) are a part of the resources of the tourism industry.

Attraction

The beauty of natural and man-made tourist destinations attracts tourists towards them. Further, places of historic and religious significance are also on the agendas of many a tourist. Water-based spots offer water skiing, parasailing and water scooter driving. Land-based spots offer skiing (on snow-clad terrain), horse riding, horse racing (for fun and betting), walking/running and visiting natural spots like gardens and zoos. Air-based spots offer hang-gliding, paragliding, bungee jumping, flying and other such activities as are related to travel in the air. All the equipment, aircraft, boats, gadgets and paraphernalia that are used to execute these activities are a part of the resources of their respective tourist organisations. In addition, historic spots, forts and palaces are also resources; these are invariably owned by the governments of these countries in which, these are located. Many of these are also would Heritage Sites. Example ; The Sun Temple of Konark (Orissa).

Transportation

Airways, roadways, waterways, cable cars, railways and pipelines are the basic modes of transport. Out of these railways, airlines, coaches, cruise lines and cable trolleys are frequently used by tourists to move from one spot to another. The aircraft, cargo handling equipment, buildings of terminals, computerised reservation systems, trucks, vans and machines used to repair the aircraft are a part of the resources of airlines. Coaches, buses, equipment used to maintain vehicles, fuel stations, machines used to lift cargo, cranes and other similar machines are the resources of road transporters. Railway engines, rolling stock, signaling systems, employees, godowns at railway stations and equipment used to transport railway cargo are the resources of a railway system. Steamships, cruise liners, equipment for handling sea cargo, vessel operators, sailors, fuel etc., are the resources of sea transport companies. Cable trolleys, ropeways, motors used to operate these trolleys and operators are the resources of the cable rope-way firms. These are available only at popular tourist resorts and not used for intracity or inter-city transport. Pipelines are not used to transport humans. Example : The coaches of Nice Tour and Travel, Kuala Lumpur.

Shopping

Tourists love to buy gifts, mementos, jewellery and other such items from the tourist spots as are typically associated with these spots. Shopping, in the context of tourism administration, has become a roaring business nowadays. All the products to be sold in shops or bazaars of tourist spots are the resources of those shop owners. The products offered by in-house shopping malls of hotels and tourist spots are also deemed resources. Further, products, eatables, cold drinks etc., sold at beaches, lakes, parks etc. are also resources of the vendors of such items. Finally, the shops and buildings in which, these products are sold are also the resources of those vendors who own such shops and buildings.

Example : A tourist may purchase the famous Feni from Panaji.

Special Characteristics

We have discussed the concept of tourism product earlier. We have also discussed, which components of the product mix are the resources for the owners and operators associated with the tourism industry. Before we study the features of the tourism product, we should study the unique features of the tourism industry, as a whole. These are as follows:—

1. Tourism is a temporary and short-term movement of tourists.
2. It involves the sale of products and services but the sale of services occupies nearly *75-80 per cent* of the garment of tourism.
3. It is an activity concerned with utilisation of leisure hours. People become tourists for the sake of fun, or to explore new areas/spots, which were hitherto unknown to them.
4. Tourism is a composite industry; its components are transport, food, beverages, bar, musical and cultural programmes, various land-based, water-based and air-based activities, fun and frolic, purchase of goods and stay in the lap of nature. The tourist may also like to confront the relics of the past during his brief sojourn at a tourist spot.

5. Business and tourism are being mixed nowadays. This feature of tourism has received attention of transporters, hotel owners, resort managers and government authorities alike.
6. Efficient planning of a tour itinerary would decide how a tourism firm would fare in the local, regional, national or global markets. As this industry essentially involves the transport of customers to the products (and not vice versa), its characteristics and marketing strategies are quite different from those that relate to marketing traditional products and services.
7. Transport is an important component of tourism. Without adequate means of transport, this industry cannot survive.

In the context of the aforementioned discussion, let us define unique features of tourism product, which are as follows :—

1. The tourism product is an intangible item. Tourists cannot taste, touch or small a tourism product. They can only "go through" package tours and enjoy experiences during the courses of such tours. They have to avail the services first and then, learn about their quality.
2. As already stated, shopping sprees of tourists lead to sales of products. So, we can state that we are selling some products to tourists. But these products are not the focus areas of tourists. Their major objective is to enjoy the environs of a tourist spot. They may or may not indulge in shopping activities. So, visit to the place of tourist interest is mandatory because they have already paid for such services. But purchase of products, eatables, gifts and souvenirs are optimal because they would buy such items only if they want to buy these.

3. Attraction plays a major role in the operations of the tourism industry. Tourists are motivated to visit tourist spots of repute because they may have heard a lot about their bewitching beauty. So, if a tourist spot or place is really attractive, it can become a hot tourist destination (provided the government, private tour operators and travel agencies give unflinching attention to it).
4. The tourism product is a complex mix of products and services. Airline, coach or railway seats, local transport modes and other vital elements, which are associated with tourism, stay and travel, are important from the viewpoint of profit generation. The complex nature of tourism product demands unique marketing strategies. It cannot be sold like Maggie Noodles from a departmental store. It must be sold by in a well-furnished office by professionals (who have been trained to execute such jobs).
5. Tourism products are invariably costly. For the residents of the West, the costs may not be very high. But for the residents of the developing and least developed nations, such costs may seem to be whopping. Air travel and cruise line travel would prove to be very costly; however, airlines offer Apex and Super Apex Fare schemes during peak holiday seasons. Tour packages are cheap if only these are booked on a twin-sharing basis. Otherwise, a package tour of 8 nights and 9 days can cost anywhere between Rs 70,000 to Rs 1,20,000, depending upon the class of travel bought and the star categories of hotels opted for stay during the itinerary.
6. Customers of a tourism product always look for quality in the tour programme or in its various components. So, the functional responsibilities of the marketing professional, in the parlance of tourism administration, increase.

7. The State is always involved in creating, preserving or developing the infrastructure related to the tourism product. Example: A private firm cannot build roads that are thousands of km in terms of length. Lakes have to be developed by the agencies of the State. Even if a private firm were engaged to execute such Herculean tasks, the government would be required to provide support of finance, electric power, right of way, equipment etc. This aspect is relevant in developing countries, though trends are changing nowadays. Finally, historic monuments, palaces, forts, gardens and zoological parks are on the priority list of the State. Example : The Archaeological Survey of India maintains several monuments in India and many sites in India have been identified as parts of World Heritage. Thus, even if the tourism industry were privatised around the world, the governments (at local and national levels) would continue to play useful soles in developing, preserving and maintaining many vital components of tourism products that are under their jurisdiction.

8. Many components of the tourism product are of perishable nature.

   Example : If the seats of an aircraft are vacant, these cannot be filled once it is airborne. The airline loses the revenue that it could have earned, had these seats been sold off to passengers. The same fact is true for cruise line and coach bookings. If hotel rooms remain unoccupied during off seasons, the hotel owner has to spend money for their maintenance, but he cannot earn money simply because these are vacant.

9. Insurance, claims management, demurrage charges, banking, Internet operations, the CRS, medical insurance and first aid facilities and infrastructure

(roads, railway systems, air networks etc.) are the components of tourism product.

10. All the elements of a tourism product mix must be synchronised in such a manner as to ensure good quality of the overall package that is being offered to the customer. Airport-hotel-airport transfers, amenities at historical sites, support of tour guides, fun and frolic activities, food, beverages, liquor etc., must be planned and a executed according to time bound schedules. This fact is true for the operations of domestic and international tourism.
11. The tourism product is designed to give pleasure to its buyer. Some other ingredients have been added to the recipe of pleasure now days, namely, research, seminars, conferences, quest for knowledge, exploration of new sites etc. But the basic purpose of delivering a tourism product is more of less the same—deriving pleasure and being relaxed at a new or beautiful spot. The modern-day man is always under stress due to the daily chores of life. He takes a break by undertaking a tour and thus, escapes from the excruciating pain of his routine life, at least for some days.
12. The customer goes to the tourism product/service; it is not delivered at his doorstep. This is a unique feature of the tourism product.
13. Customers of tourism products are heterogeneous people. They can be rich, poor, whimsical, always in a hurry, very slow, egoists, very old, little children and even executives in their mid-forties. They may feel uncomfortable when they are huddled together in groups and taken to various tourist spots. If group tourism activities are executed, their personalised needs are given a back-seat, but that is quite natural. Group tours are cheaper than personalised

(individual) tours. However, tourism marketers must try to understand the precise needs of each and every tourist in a group and make efforts to satisfy those needs to the maximum possible extent. While doing so, however, they must not forget the constraints that have been imposed on them by time, resources, tour itineraries and the tourism organisation they work for.

CHAPTER–2

NEW CONCEPTS

There has been an upmarket trend in the tourism over the last few decades, especially in Europe, where international travel for short breaks is common. Tourists have high levels of disposable income, considerable leisure time, are well educated, and have sophisticated tastes. There is now a demand for a better quality products, which has resulted in a fragmenting of the mass market for beach vacations; people want more specialised versions, quieter resorts, family-oriented holidays or niche market-targeted destination hotels.

The developments in technology and transport infrastructure, such as jumbo jets, low-cost airlines and more accessible airports have made many types of tourism more affordable. WHO estimates that up to 500,000 people are on planes at any time. There have also been changes in lifestyle, such as retiree-age people who sustain year round tourism. This is facilitated by internet sales of tourism products. Some sites have now started to offer dynamic packaging, in which an inclusive price is quoted for a tailor-made package requested by the customer upon impulse.

There have been a few setbacks in tourism, such as the September 11 attacks and terrorist threats to tourist destinations, such as in Bali and several European cities. Also, on December 26, 2004, a tsunami, caused by the 2004 Indian

Ocean earthquake, hit the Asian countries on the Indian Ocean, including the Maldives. Thousands of lives were lost and many tourists died. This, together with the vast clean-up operation in place, has stopped or severely hampered tourism to the area.

The terms *tourism* and *travel* are sometimes used interchangeably. In this context, travel has a similar definition to tourism, but implies a more purposeful journey. The terms *tourism* and *tourist* are sometimes used pejoratively, to imply a shallow interest in the cultures or locations visited by tourists.

Sustainable Tourism

"Sustainable tourism is envisaged as leading to management of all resources in such a way that economic, social and aesthetic needs can be fulfilled while maintaining cultural integrity, essential ecological processes, biological diversity and life support systems." (World Tourism Organization)

Sustainable development implies "meeting the needs of the present without compromising the ability of future generations to meet their own needs" (World Commission on Environment and Development, 1987)

Sustainable tourism can be seen as having regard to ecological and socio-cultural carrying capacities and includes involving the community of the destination in tourism development planning. It also involves integrating tourism to match current economic and growth policies so as to mitigate some of the negative economic and social impacts of 'mass tourism'. Murphy (1985) advocates the use of an 'ecological approach', to consider both 'plants' and 'people' when implementing the sustainable tourism development process. This is in contrast to the 'boosterism' and 'economic' approaches to tourism planning, neither of which consider the detrimental ecological or sociological impacts of tourism development to a destination.

However, Butler (2006) questions the exposition of the term 'sustainable' in the context of tourism, citing its ambiguity and stating that "the emerging sustainable development philosophy of the 1990s can be viewed as an extension of the broader realization that a preoccupation with economic growth without regard to it social and environmental consequences is self-defeating in the long term." Thus 'sustainable tourism development' is seldom considered as an autonomous function of economic regeneration as separate from general economic growth.

Ecotourism

Ecotourism, also known as ecological tourism, is responsible travel to fragile, pristine, and usually protected areas that strives to be low impact and (often) small scale. It helps educate the traveler; provides funds for conservation; directly benefits the economic development and political empowerment of local communities; and fosters respect for different cultures and for human rights.

Pro-poor Tourism

The pro poor tourism has to help the very poorest in developing countries has been receiving increasing attention by those involved in development and the issue has been addressed either through small scale projects in local communities and by Ministries of Tourism attempting to attract huge numbers of tourists. Research by the Overseas Development Institute suggests that neither is the best way to encourage tourists' money to reach the poorest as only 25% or less (far less in some cases) ever reaches the poor; successful examples of money reaching the poor include mountain climbing in Tanzania or cultural tourism in Luang Prabang, Laos.

Recession Tourism

Recession tourism is a travel trend, which evolved by way of the world economic crisis. Identified by American entrepreneur Matt Landau (2007), recession tourism is defined by low-cost, high-value experiences taking place of once-popular generic retreats. Various recession tourism hotspots have seen business boom during the recession thanks to comparatively low costs of living and a slow world job market suggesting travelers are elongating trips where their money travels further.

Medical Tourism

When there is a significant price difference between countries for a given medical procedure, particularly in Southeast Asia, India, Eastern Europe and where there are different regulatory regimes, in relation to particular medical procedures (e.g. dentistry), traveling to take advantage of the price or regulatory differences is often referred to as "medical tourism".

Educational Tourism

Educational tourism developed, because of the growing popularity of teaching and learning of knowledge and the enhancing of technical competency outside of the classroom environment. In educational tourism, the main focus of the tour or leisure activity includes visiting another country to learn about the culture, such as in Student Exchange Programs and Study Tours, or to work and apply skills learned inside the classroom in a different environment, such as in the International Practicum Training Program.

Creative Tourism

Creative tourism has existed as a form of cultural tourism, since the early beginnings of tourism itself. Its European roots date back to the time of the Grand Tour, which saw the sons of aristocratic families traveling for the purpose of mostly interactive, educational experiences. More recently, creative tourism has been given its own name by Crispin Raymond and Greg Richards, who as members of the Association for Tourism and Leisure Education (ATLAS), have directed a number of projects for the European Commission, including cultural and crafts tourism, known as sustainable tourism. They have defined "creative tourism" as tourism related to the active participation of travellers in the culture of the host community, through interactive workshops and informal learning experiences.

Meanwhile, the concept of creative tourism has been picked up by high-profile organizations such as UNESCO, who through the Creative Cities Network, have endorsed creative tourism as an engaged, authentic experience that promotes an active understanding of the specific cultural features of a place.

More recently, creative tourism has gained popularity as a form of cultural tourism, drawing on active participation by travelers in the culture of the host communities they visit. Several countries offer examples of this type of tourism development, including the United Kingdom, the Bahamas, Jamaica, Spain, Italy and New Zealand.

Dark Tourism

One emerging area of special interest has been identified by Lennon and Foley (2000) as "dark" tourism. This type of tourism involves visits to "dark" sites, such as battlegrounds, scenes of horrific crimes or acts of genocide, for example: concentration camps. Dark tourism remains a small niche market, driven by varied motivations, such as mourning, remembrance, education, macabre curiosity or even entertainment. Its early origins are rooted in fairgrounds and medieval fairs.

Doom Tourism

Also known as "Tourism of Doom," or "Last Chance Tourism" this emerging trend involves traveling to places that are environmentally or otherwise threatened (the ice caps of Mount Kilimanjaro, the melting glaciers of Patagonia, The coral of the Great Barrier Reef) before it is too late. Identified by travel trade magazine TravelAge West editor-in-chief Kenneth Shapiro in 2007 and later explored in The New York Times, this type of tourism is believed to be on the rise. Some see the trend as related to sustainable tourism or ecotourism due to the fact that a number of these tourist destinations are considered threatened by environmental factors such as global warming, over population or climate change. Others worry that travel to many of these threatened locations increases an individual's carbon footprint and only hastens problems threatened locations are already facing.

Growth

The World Tourism Organization (UNWTO) forecasts that international tourism will continue growing at the average annual rate of 4 %. With the advent of e-commerce, tourism products have become one of the most traded items on the internet. Tourism products and services have been made available through intermediaries, although tourism providers (hotels, airlines, etc.) can sell their services directly. This has put pressure on intermediaries from both on-line and traditional shops.

It has been suggested there is a strong correlation between tourism expenditure per capita and the degree to which countries play in the global context. Not only as a result of the important economic contribution of the tourism industry, but also as an indicator of the degree of confidence with which global citizens leverage the resources of the globe for the benefit of their local economies. This is why any projections of growth in tourism may serve as an indication of the relative influence that each country will exercise in the future.

Space tourism is expected to "take off" in the first quarter of the 21st century, although compared with traditional destinations the number of tourists in orbit will remain low until technologies such as a space elevator make space travel cheap.

Technological improvement is likely to make possible air-ship hotels, based either on solar-powered airplanes or large dirigibles. Underwater hotels, such as Hydropolis, expected to open in Dubai in 2009, will be built. On the ocean, tourists will be welcomed by ever larger cruise ships and perhaps floating cities.

Sports Tourism

Since the late 1970s, sports tourism has become increasingly popular. Events such as rugby, Olympics, Commonwealth games, Asian Games and football World Cups have enabled specialist travel companies to gain official ticket allocation and then sell them in packages that include flights, hotels and excursions.

Latest Trends

As a result of the late-2000s recession, international arrivals suffered a strong slowdown beginning in June 2008. Growth from 2007 to 2008 was only 3.7% during the first eight months of 2008. The Asian and Pacific markets were affected and Europe stagnated during the boreal summer months, while the Americas performed better, reducing their expansion rate but keeping a 6% growth from January to August 2008. Only the Middle East continued its rapid growth during the same period, reaching a 17% growth as compared to the same period in 2007. This slowdown on international tourism demand was also reflected in the air transport industry, with a negative growth in September 2008 and a 3.3% growth in passenger traffic through September. The hotel industry also reports a slowdown, as room occupancy continues to decline. As the global economic situation deteriorated dramatically during September and October as a result of the global financial crisis, growth of international tourism is expected to slow even further for the remaining of 2008, and this slowdown in demand growth is forecasted to continue into 2009 as recession has already hit most of the top spender countries, with long-haul travel expected to be the most affected by the economic crisis. This negative trend intensified as international tourist arrivals fell by 8% during the first four months of 2009, and the decline was exacerbated in some regions due to the outbreak of the influenza AH1N1 virus.

Human Right

On the 15th of April 2010 a headline in the British newspaper, *The Sunday Times*, proclaimed that European Commissioner Antonio Tajani had unveiled a plan declaring tourism a human right. According to the article itself: Tajani's view is that pensioners, youths and those too poor to afford it should have their travel subsidised by the taxpayer. Tajani's program will be piloted until 2013 and then put into full operation. In introducing his plan, Tajani stated, "Travelling for tourism today is a right. The way we spend our holidays is a formidable indicator of our quality of life." His spokesman added, "Why should someone from the Mediterranean not be able to travel to Edinburgh in summer for a breath of cool, fresh air; why should someone from Edinburgh not be able to travel to Greece in winter?" The characterization of Tajani's position as advocating an expansion of human rights was repeated by other media such as the conservative Canadian newspaper National Post and Wikipedia. According to Euractive it proved impossible for the commissioner's office to correct the misleading impression created by the *Sunday Times* headline in the

Wikipedia articles on tourism and Antonio Tajani as the *Sunday Times* is a "reliable published source" while the actual text of the Commissioner's speech is only a "primary source".

EurActiv, an independent media portal, criticized the article by *The Sunday Times* as an example of misleading information about the EU which appears in the British press and then picked up by other Anglo-Saxon media and blogs, and Wikipedia. EurActiv notes that "the article on *The Sunday Times* never quotes the Commissioner as having made such a statement. Nevertheless, it pursues the argument under the headline "Brussels decrees holidays as a human right," underlining the alleged "hundreds of millions of pounds" that pursuing the idea would cost taxpayers." EurActiv criticized Wikipedia on the grounds that it proved impossible for Commissioner Tajani's team to correct the wrong information in the encyclopedia, and echoed European Commission spokesperson Pia Ahrenkilde Hansen's statement that "ethics in digital communications is definitely a subject which deserves to be addressed."

CHAPTER-3

PLANNING AND DEVELOPMENT

Planning is the dynamic process of determining goals, systematically selecting alternative courses of actions to achieve those goals, implementing the chosen alternatives and evaluating the choice to determine if it if successful. The planning process regards the environment which includes political, physical, social and economic elements as interrelated and interdependent components which should be taken into account in considering the future of a destination area.

Tourism is one of many activities in a community or region that requires planning and coordination. This bulletin provides a simple structure and basic guidelines for comprehensive tourism planning at a community or regional level. Planning is the process of identifying objectives and defining and evaluating methods of achieving them. By comprehensive planning we mean planning which considers all of the tourism resources, organizations, markets, and programs within a region. Comprehensive planning also considers economic, environmental, social, and institutional aspects of tourism development.

Tourism planning has evolved from two related but distinct sets of planning philosophies and methods. On the one hand, tourism is one of many activities in an area that must be considered as part of physical, environmental, social, and economic planning. Therefore, it is common to find tourism addressed, at least partially, in a regional land use, transportation, recreation, economic development, or comprehensive plan. The degree to which tourism is addressed in such plans depends upon the relative importance of tourism to the community or region and how sensitive the planning authority is to tourism activities.

Tourism may also be viewed as a business in which a community or region chooses to engage. Individual tourism businesses conduct a variety of planning activities including feasibility, marketing, product development, promotion, forecasting, and strategic planning. If tourism is a significant component of an area's economy or development plans, regional or community-wide marketing plans are needed to coordinate the development and marketing activities of different tourism interests in the community.

A comprehensive approach integrates a strategic marketing plan with more traditional public planning activities. This ensures a balance between serving the needs and wants of the tourists versus the needs and wants of local residents. A formal tourism plan provides a vehicle for the various interests within a community to coordinate their activities and work toward common goals. It also is a means of coordinating tourism with other community activities.

Planned Development

The serious situation caused by haphazard development has made people and the governments aware of the need for planning of tourism development based on scientific research of the requirements of the travel market and the capacity of the area to take in the tourists. The need for planning is paramount. We do not provide more seats to a plane or rooms in a hotel beyond its maximum capacity, taking into account the passenger's comforts. Why should a resort or an area be choked with people?

Planning of tourism development, however, is of recent origin. It was specially taken note of during the last 65 years after public voices were heard against the unplanned invasion of tourism. In 1950, Gerhard Noble called mass tourism "one of the great western plagues hardly less evil in effects than the epidemics of the middle ages." In a conference held in Limuru, Kenya, the tourist inflow was referred to "as a dangerous invasion." These remarks, however, may be exaggerated apprehensions of the environmentalists. But no one disputes the fact that where modern industrial life makes inroads into ancient societies, traditional values begin to totter. Tourism is a form of social industrialisation with all its advantages and disadvantages. Its advantages have to be grasped and utilised with care so that the impact of the disadvantages is minimised. It is here that planning comes in. Planning is of greater benefit to developing societies where tourism is a new phenomenon and has had little or no adverse effect so far. The World Bank warned us as early as 1972:

In many areas of the world, tourism development has produced great disparities in the standards of amenities provided for the visitors and for the local population. This cannot be entirely avoided, but in the long run, the improvement of standards for the local population is probably a condition of successful tourism development. The development of a new resort by the provision of infrastructure costing perhaps millions of dollars has a great impact on land values in the area affected. Were these benefits to accrue largely to a few private landowners, the Bank would have difficulty in financing such a project. The acquisition of land by government or a public agency prior to development... eases the problems of planning on an integrated basis, and of enforcing proper zoning and building regulations. It also helps to ensure that windfall gains do not accrue solely to private landowners and provides the opportunity for the public agency to offer serviced sites to hotel developers at prices which can include, if necessary, an incentive element. There is a very close relationship between land prices and building densities, and by appropriate land pricing the development authority can help to ensure that acceptable physical planning and density standards are maintained.

The statement makes two significant points:

1. Planning should be integrated to avoid as far as possible, disparities in the standards of amenities for the visitors and local population.
2. Tourism planning should not be left totally to private enterprise in search of profit. Government must actively participate in it.

In the past, tourism planning was looked at from a simplistic point of view. Planning simply implied that new hotel construction should be encouraged, more airlines should start operation, promotional campaigns may be launched within the country and abroad and border crossing must be eased. Although it worked to some extent, it was at best an erratic method of planning tourism. That is how most developing countries started their own tourism planning, resulting in a number of mistakes.

Tourism has become a major industry in many countries of the world and has thus a pervasive effect on the economy of the nations as well as their social structure. Unplanned tourism can hamper a nation in getting maximum benefits from its development.

The development of the tourism sector is one of the several options before a government, making claims on its resources which, in most cases, are limited. It is, therefore, necessary for tourism planners to place their case before the government in justifiable terms listing anticipated contribution to the economic development of the country through tourism development. The two economic arguments in favour of developing tourism are:

1. the contribution in terms of foreign exchange; and
2. multiple employment potential of the tourism industry. Tourism development has to be planned in relation to the total development of the country and the available resources.

Initially, in the fifties and sixties, most countries except USA were interested in measuring international tourism because this was what mattered to them in economic terms. Meanwhile, USA and subsequently Europe discovered the value of domestic tourism. Its effect on economy was as good as international tourism. In fact, it provided more regional balance than international tourism. In several countries, an annual survey of domestic tourism is conducted and its findings are available to travel industry. Similarly, US Database, a travel research organisation of the USA, has been gathering all kinds of data on domestic and international tourism for more than two decades.

Presently, almost all National Tourist Organisations in developing countries have divisions dealing with domestic tourism. But, only feeble attempts have been made to quantify domestic tourism. For instance, the Government of India has not yet ordered an all-India survey to determine the size and magnitude of domestic tourism. A few Tourism Departments of the State Governments have set up their research sections to quantify the size of domestic tourism in their states.

The following are some reasons for the need of statistical measurement of tourism:

1. Statistical measurement is necessary to evaluate scale and magnitude of tourism to a destination. It can relate to a country, region or a city. The research helps a country forecast future demand over a long period—say, ten years.
2. The results of these researches are important to take decisions relating to physical planning and area

development, keeping in view the requirements of the visitors and the local population. In the absence of timely research, a lot more investments will be needed for future expansion. In the sixties, the Government of India built a new airport in Calcutta and by the time it was completed, it was already short of requirements. It was built without adequate research on future demand.

3. Statistical information is required for marketing and destination promotion. The people in charge of marketing want to know which are their prime markets, how market profiles change, information about the emerging new markets, etc.

Process of Planning

Tourism is part of the services industry. Its importance—economic and social — has to be balanced by a government in relation to the competing priorities of a nation.

A government must take a decision as to whether tourism is important for its economic, social and political interests. And, if the decision is positive, planning based on indepth research is imperative. The economic advantages of tourism are so overpowering that decision in most cases has been favourable. The erstwhile USSR under Joseph Stalin was forbidden to foreign visitors till 1960, but it opened up with a vengeance when Stalin died. The new Russian state immediately switched to international tourism to get its share of the tourist dollar. Other East European states and the newly independent Republics which once-formed part of the Soviet Union are now trying to attract travellers. China was a closed society a decade ago. Now, it is one of the top 15 among the tourist receiving countries, thanks to the massive foreign investments it received from multi-national companies.

While tourism planning is usually thought in terms of developers and promoters in specific projects, it must be seen from national, regional and local levels. Tourism planning and development has to be seen from two levels:

1. The geographical level within which the tourism activity occurs — the destination.
2. At the level of individual operator — resort or a hotel.

Steps in the Planning Process

Like any planning, tourism planning is goal-oriented, striving to achieve certain objectives by matching available resources and programs with the needs and wants of people. Comprehensive planning requires a systematic approach, usually involving a series of steps. The process is best viewed as an iterative and on-going one, with each step subject to modification and refinement at any stage of the planning process.

There are six steps in the planning process:

1. Define goals and objectives.
2. Identify the tourism system.
   (a) Resources
   (b) Organizations
   (c) Markets
3. Generate alternatives.
4. Evaluate alternatives.
5. Select and implement.
6. Monitor and evaluate.

Step One: Defining Goals and objectives. Obtaining clear statements of goals and objectives is difficult, but important. Ideally, tourism development goals should flow from more general community goals and objectives. It is important to understand how a tourism plan serves these broader purposes. Is the community seeking a broader tax base, increased employment opportunities, expanded recreation facilities, better educational programs, a higher quality of life? How can tourism contribute to these objectives?

If tourism is identified as a means of serving broader community goals, it makes sense to develop plans with more specific tourism development objectives. These are generally defined through a continuing process in which various groups and organizations in a community work together toward common goals. A local planning authority, chamber of commerce, visitors bureau, or similar group should assume a leadership role to develop an initial plan and obtain broad involvement of tourism interests in the community. Public support for the planning process and plan is also important.

Having a good understanding of tourism and the tourism system in your community is the first step toward defining goals and objectives for tourism development. The types of goals that are appropriate and the precision with which you are able to define them will depend upon how long your community has been involved in tourism and tourism planning.

In the early stages of tourism development, goals may involve establishing organizational structures and collecting information to better identify the tourism system in the community. Later, more precise objectives can be formulated and more specific development and marketing strategies evaluated.

Step Two: Identifying Your Tourism System When planning for any type of activity, it is important to first define its scope and characteristics. Be clear about exactly what your plan encompasses. A good initial question is, "What do you mean by tourism?" Tourism is defined in many ways. Generally, tourism involves people traveling outside of their community for pleasure. Definitions differ on the specifics of how far people must travel, whether or not they must stay overnight, for how long, and what exactly is included under traveling for "pleasure". Do you want your tourism plan to include day visitors, conventioneers, business travelers, people visiting friends and relatives, people passing through, or seasonal residents?

Which community resources and organizations serve tourists or could serve tourists? Generally, tourists share community resources with local residents and businesses. Many organizations serve both tourists and locals. This complicates tourism planning and argues for a clear idea of what your tourism plan entails.

You can begin to clarify the tourism system by breaking it down into three subsystems:

1. tourism resources,
2. tourism organizations, and
3. tourism markets.

An initial task in developing a tourism plan is to identify, inventory, and classify the objects within each of these subsystems.

Influencing Factors

The following are some of the factors which influence tourism development in a destination area:

1. Size of the existing population.
2. Diversity and vitality of already existing tourist activity.
3. Whether the facilities were planned and planted in the area or grew spontaneously because of some man-made or national attraction.
4. Availability of land and finance.
5. Impact on the local community—benefits and social costs.
6. Attitude of the local people towards the tourism projects.

7. Magnitude and speed of development.
8. State of the local economy — options of alternate development.
9. Availability of local manpower — a dynamic population.
10. Whether the area is extensive for future expansion or only limited expansion is possible.

Resentment by local population against tourism projects, however beneficial to the community, can create problems, as it happened in Australia. Yeppon is a small town on the coast of central Queensland—Australia's sunshine state described by its 6,000 inhabitants as 'Paradise'. It has beautiful views and miles of glorious beaches. A Japanese businessman saw the area and fell in love with it, deciding to develop it into a resort. The beach here is 10 times longer and wider than Waikiki in Honolulu. He bought 20,000 acres to develop it into an international resort, building a number of hotels, guest houses, wildlife parks and several other attractive features.

The scheme was approved by the Australian Government but the local residents did not like it. They could not tolerate the idea of thousands of tourists crowding their beaches all the year round.

The investor tried to woo the local population, offering them millions of dollars to build a retirement home and other facilities. In November 1981, a bomb exploded under a motel under construction destroying property.

This is an example of the type of problems a developer can face — if local cooperation is not sought.

Planning Levels

Planning has to be done on two levels — national and local. At the national level, the central government will be involved in developing selected areas on the basis of research and study. The guiding principles in the selection of the areas are their marketability as tourist spots to international and domestic travellers, anticipated receipts from the tourism sector, and projections of future demand. The national plan shall also lay down the broad framework for development at local and regional levels.

The detailed planning of the local needs has to be done at the local level though the central government may give financial assistance or subsidies to some of the activities. This arrangement is prevalent in countries where tourism is not highly developed and the state has to play a pivotal role. In India, although the government is involved in tourism planning, the private sector plays a significant role in developing tourist facilities. Some of the facilities are planned, developed and managed solely by the state. Now, most countries including China have opened their tourism sector for private participation.

It may, however, be understood that a government cannot afford to do everything at once. They have to select priority areas for development where some infrastructure may exist and whose tourist attractions are relatively better known. The development of completely new areas, though a worthwhile proposition in time, has to take its turn depending upon the resources of the country and the political will to develop tourism on the part of the government.

In October 1977, the World Tourism Organisation published an inventory of tourism development plans of various countries. Out of the forty-three member-countries, which replied to the WTO questionnaire, thirty-seven had an integrated planning system at the national level. But in majority of the cases, the plans remained on paper and when these were acted upon, action was half-hearted or partial implementation. Some countries, like the United States and Canada, have, strictly speaking, no national tourism plans. In the USA, a study for making federal policy and programme involvement in tourism more coherent and responsive to national interest was undertaken only in 1976. After six years of intensive efforts by the travel industry, President Ronald Reagan signed into law a National Tourism Policy Act on October 16,1981. Under this Act, the US Congress created the US Travel and Tourism Administration to 'optimise' the contribution of tourism and recreation industries to economic prosperity, full employment and international balance of payments to the US. In 1996 USTTA has been axed in an economy drive by Clinton Administration. In Canada, each of the ten provinces and two territories are involved in tourism development planning. In USA, states are more actively involved in the promotion of tourism even more than the federal government. France has a full-fledged Ministry of Free Time which deals with tourism and leisure affairs.

Integrated Planning

There has been little coordination and regulation in physical planning for tourism development. Resorts have developed in attractive settings while ancillary facilities like transportation were created belatedly to meet the demand. Industrial and commercial cities found themselves receiving more visitors. The new, substantial facilities created were shared by foreign visitors and the local people. Existing infrastructure designed for the requirements of a relatively static age came under the strain of a new and mobile society. The need for replanning of the existing use of land and planning of new areas became paramount. This realisation, however, came only in the second half of the twentieth century. Simultaneously, the transport revolution opened new parts of the world for touristic exploration.

The tourism planners, therefore, had two different tasks — one of physical planning in new areas with potential but with little or no existing touristic activity, and the other of re-shaping the areas where tourism already existed. Two, replanning of existing high density tourist areas.

Where should the planners begin? The first thing is to analyse different types of national or other tourist resources — of which each country has many — that could attract tourists. These may be of scenic beauty, history, a mystique, and so on. An inventory of all these resources of the country has to be made. Then, there are cities like London and Paris which have their own natural draw for visitors. London, the biggest tourist attraction in the world, is visited by over 10 million tourists and Paris by about 20 million foreign visitors annually.

After preparing the inventory, areas have to be selected for tourism development keeping in view the economic resources available. While taking up the areas for development in a city, it is necessary to define the minimum urban planning parameters which, if respected, may prevent the degradation of the environment through unregulated building activity. The Mediterranean seacoast is an example of such unregulated development leading to ugliness and confusion.

The basic parameters in planning a sea resort should indicate (a) the space between buildings, (b) the distance of the road from the beach; and (c) the capacity of tourist accommodation on the beach or off the beach.

The guidelines should also give building specifications, length, suggested dimensions, and characteristics of the road network providing access to the sea. The creation and development of a green belt should be clearly marked. No unregulated or unplanned structures should be allowed in the area proposed to be developed. Similarly, the tourism development plan of an area with historical monuments as a major attraction requires that the view of the monuments should not be concealed by any haphazard construction in the area surrounding the, monument. For instance, no new construction should be allowed near the Taj Mahal, which may obstruct its view.

To sum up, the following must be considered in any area planning:

1. Preparation of overall inventory of national tourist resources.
2. Determination of broad parameters of urban planning and architectural specifications.
3. Cost benefit studies of the proposed projects.
4. Exploration of possibilities of investment in private and public sectors.

Investment and Income in Tourism Development : When a tourism project is taken up for implementation, the time relation between investment requirements and revenue expectation has to be kept in mind. The chart on this relationship and the involvement of the public sector in this chapter explains the position.

The following 8-point project structure for tourism planning and development is recommended:

1. Establishment of goals after a feasibility study.
2. Market and resources analysis.
3. Conceptual planning.
4. Approval of the plan.
5. Master planning.
6. Staged implementation programme.
7. Evaluation and direction.
8. Monitoring operations to ensure quality of services and operational success.

Systems must be set up to provide continuing feedback on volume of tourism and levels of satisfaction provided. Such programmes are directed against decline of a destination.

Improved Environmental Management and Planning

Sound environmental management of tourism facilities and especially hotels can increase the benefits to natural areas. But this requires careful planning for controlled development, based on analysis of the environmental resources of the area. Planning helps to make choices between conflicting uses, or to find ways to make them compatible. By planning early for tourism development, damaging and expensive mistakes can be prevented, avoiding the gradual deterioration of environmental assets significant to tourism.

Cleaner production techniques can be important tools for planning and operating tourism facilities in a way that minimizes their environmental impacts. For example, green building (using energy-efficient and non-polluting construction materials, sewage systems and energy sources) is an increasingly important way for the tourism industry to decrease its impact on the environment. And because waste treatment and disposal are often major, long-term environmental problems in the tourism industry, pollution prevention and waste minimization techniques are especially important for the tourism industry. A guide to sources of information on cleaner production (free) is available here.

Environmental Awareness Raising

Tourism has the potential to increase public appreciation of the environment and to spread awareness of environmental problems when it brings people into closer contact with nature and the environment. This confrontation may heighten awareness of the value of nature and lead to environmentally conscious behavior and activities to preserve the environment. For instance, Honduran schoolchildren from the capital city of Tegucigalpa are routinely taken to visit La Tigra cloud forest visitor center, funded in part by eco-tourist dollars, to learn about the intricacies of the rainforest.

If it is to be sustainable in the long run, tourism must incorporate the principles and practices of sustainable consumption. Sustainable consumption includes building consumer demand for products that have been made using cleaner production techniques, and for services - including tourism services - that are provided in a way that minimizes environmental impacts. The tourism industry can play a key role in providing environmental information and raising awareness among tourists of the environmental consequences of their actions. Tourists and tourism-related businesses consume an enormous quantity of goods and services; moving them toward using those that are produced and provided in an environmentally sustainable way, from cradle to grave, could have an enormous positive impact on the planet's environment.

Protection and Preservation

Tourism can significantly contribute to environmental protection, conservation and restoration of biological diversity and sustainable use of natural resources. Because of their attractiveness, pristine sites and natural areas are identified as valuable and the need to keep the attraction alive can lead to creation of national parks and wildlife parks.

In Hawaii, new laws and regulations have been enacted to preserve the Hawaiian rainforest and to protect native species. The coral reefs around the islands and the marine life that depend on them for survival are also protected. Hawaii now has become an international center for research on ecological systems - and the promotion and preservation of the islands' tourism industry was the main motivation for these actions. (Source: Mundus)

Grupo Punta Cana, a resort in the Dominican Republic, offers an example of how luxury tourism development and conservation can be combined. The high-end resort was established with the goal of catering to luxury-class tourists while respecting the natural habitat of Punta Cana. The developers have set aside 10,000 hectares (24,700 acres) of land as a nature reserve and native fruit tree garden. The Punta Cana Nature Reserve includes 11 fresh water springs surrounded by a subtropical forest where many species of unusual Caribbean flora and fauna live in their natural state. Guests can explore a "nature path" leading from the beach through mangroves, lagoons of fresh water springs and dozens of species of Caribbean bird and plant life. The Punta Cana Ecological Foundation has begun reforesting some parts of the reserve that had been stripped of their native mahogany and other trees in the past. Other environmentally protective policies have been put into effect at the resort, such as programs to protect the offshore barrier reefs and the recycling of wastewater for use in irrigating the grounds. The fairways of the resort's new golf course were planted with a hybrid grass that can be irrigated with sea water The grass also requires less than half the usual amounts of fertilizer and pesticides. The resort has also established a biodiversity laboratory run by Cornell University.

Tourism has had a positive effect on wildlife preservation and protection efforts, notably in Africa but also in South America, Asia, Australia, and the South Pacific. Numerous animal and plant species have already become extinct or may become extinct soon. Many countries have therefore established wildlife reserves and enacted strict laws protecting the animals that draw nature-loving tourists. As a result of these measures, several endangered species have begun to thrive again.

Alternative Employment

Tourism can provide an alternative to development scenarios that may have greater environmental impacts. The Eco-escuela de Español, a Spanish language school created in 1996 as part of a Conservation International project in the Guatemalan village of San Andres, is an example. The community-owned school, located in the Maya Biosphere Reserve, combines individual language courses with home stay opportunities and community-led eco-tours. It receives around 1,800 tourists yearly, mostly from the US and Europe, and employs almost 100 residents, of whom around 60% were previously engaged in mostly illegal timber extraction, hunting and *milpas*, or slash-and-burn agriculture. Careful monitoring in 2000 has shown that, among the families benefiting from the business, the majority has significantly reduced hunting practices, and the number and extension of "slash-and-burn" agricultural plots. Furthermore, as most families in the village benefit directly or indirectly from the school, community-managed private reserves have been established, and social pressure against hunting has increased.

Regulatory Measures

Regulatory measures help offset negative impacts; for instance, controls on the number of tourist activities and movement of visitors within protected areas can limit impacts on the ecosystem and help maintain the integrity and vitality of the site. Such limits can also reduce the negative impacts on resources.

Limits should be established after an in-depth analysis of the maximum sustainable visitor capacity. This strategy is being used in the Galapagos Islands, where the number of ships allowed to cruise this remote archipelago is limited, and only designated islands can be visited, ensuring visitors have little impact on the sensitive environment and animal habitats.

Effects of Other Industries on Tourism

Impacts from other industries often have a more dramatic effect on the environment and can seriously affect tourism.

1. Oil spills, like the oil tanker disaster that occurred off the Galapagos Islands (Ecuador) in January 2001, can cause severe short-term damage to tourist

attractions. In that case, a freight ship loaded with 160,000 gallons of diesel fuel and 80,000 gallons of other petroleum products ran aground on the coast of San Cristóbal and spilled nearly all of its load. Unique local marine and land species and the tourism potential of the area were badly affected.

2. Agricultural runoff or industrial discharges can cause water pollution and may cause algae blooms like those that occurred in the Adriatic Sea in the early 1990s. In spite of improved control of sewage from tourism developments, the Mediterranean sea floor is increasingly carpeted with these quick-growing invaders, many rising 30 inches or more above anchoring runners. They appear equally adept at colonizing rock, mud, and sand in a virtually continuous swath that can extend from the beach out to a depth of about 150 feet, smothering coral reefs, fish and other sea flora and fauna in the process.
3. Destructive practices such as blast fishing, fishing with poisonous chemicals like cyanide, and muro-ami netting (pounding reefs with weighted bags to scare fish out of crevices) directly destroy corals. They can also destroy a major draw for tourists.

Environmental Standards and Infrastructure Increasingly Determine Competitiveness

Environmental protection, along with a modern transport infrastructure, are the factors which are increasingly determining the competitiveness of international destinations in the market for travel and tourism. Countries which include tourism more strongly in sustainable overall concepts can strengthen their position. That is one of the findings of the Global Travel & Tourism Competitiveness Report 2008 (TTCR). This second edition of the annual report has been prepared by the World Economic Forum in conjunction with the international strategy and technology consultants Booz & Company and other well-known partners. The report lists the 130 countries studied on an index assessing their competitiveness in the travel and tourism sector.

Recommendations from the last report were well-received by decision-makers in the tourism and tourist travel sectors; this is partly reflected in the form of practical changes whose effects can also be noted in the new ranking. Switzerland, Austria and Germany continue to top the list, particularly on account of their environmental standards (exemplary in international terms) and similarly exemplary transport infrastructure. Sweden has achieved a significant leap of nine places up the rankings, partly due to its heightened efforts on environmental issues. These same concerns also account for the good index rankings achieved by the other Scandinavian countries. Improvements are also noted for Brazil (up 10 places) and for two Mediterranean states, Spain (up 10 places) and Italy (up 5 places). Progress has also been achieved by other popular Southern European holiday destinations, such as Portugal (up 7 places) and Greece (up 5 places).

The Travel and Tourism Sector as the Driver of Regulatory Changes

A further finding of this report is that the travel and tourism sector is a key wealth driver for emerging countries like China and South Africa. These nations have used supportive legislation to decisively improve their competitiveness in these areas. China, which this year is staging the Olympic Games, achieved dramatic improvements in the ranking,, due to a combination or regulatory adjustments and infrastructure measures (up to 62nd in the ranking from 71 last year). South Africa also succeeded in moving up the rankings (to 60th spot, up from

62 last year); the country is set to be the first on the African continent to stage the Football World Cup, in 2010.

Countries with a Long-term Environmental Agenda Prominently Ranked

Countries placing a stronger emphasis on sustainability come out particularly well in the rankings, and Bulgaria is a good example of this. The country has developed concepts offering alternatives to package holiday tourism on the Black Sea coast. "Implementing strategies is one of the most important success factors in establishing a balance between short-term economic successes and long-term ecological objectives," says Jürgen Ringbeck, a managing partner with Booz & Company. He adds that customers will increasingly demand "green" tourism services. "The travel and tourism companies are now faced with the challenge of satisfying this demand."

EU States Amongst the Most Competitive when it Comes to Tourism

As a consequence of their advanced infrastructure, secure statutory framework conditions and high level of education and training, the industrialised nations again come out best in the ranking. Amongst the Top 10 of the total number of 130 countries studied for the TTCR, there is strong representation from Europe, which accounts for seven of the places. In addition to Switzerland (1), Austria (2) and Germany (3), the leading group includes Spain (5), Great Britain (6), Sweden (8) and France (10). Italy improved on its poor ranking of the previous year, rising to 28th spot in this year's index. However, in the European comparison this popular holiday destination continues to lag behind due to the high price level, relatively low safety standards and, above all, the poorly-developed mind-set in terms of protecting the environment.

The Study – approach Adopted and Presentation

In total, 130 countries around the world were studied, looking at over 60 variables. These included taking account of statutory regulations, health and safety, infrastructure, the local price level and cultural aspects. To acknowledge the growing influence of the environmental protection factor in tourism and tourist travel, the index was expanded to include specific analysis of the points "ecology and sustainability".

The full report can be downloaded at the World Economic Forum's homepage:

The results of the TCCR are being presented in detail at the ITB in Berlin. On 7 March 2008, a panel discussion is being held in Hall 7.1a between 15:00 and 16:00. Using comparative country analyses, the event and presentation will illustrate those factors which increase a country's competitiveness and the business decisions which ought to be derived from that evidence. Following the event, the speakers will be available to conduct more in-depth discussions.

CHAPTER–4

TOURISM MARKETING

Tourism marketing is defined in a number of ways. It could be defined as the "systematic and coordinated efforts exerted by the National Tourist Organisations and/or the - tourist enterprises at international, national and local levels to optimise the satisfaction of tourists, groups and individuals, in view of the sustained tourism growth."

According to Krippendorf, J., marketing in tourism means "systematic and coordinated execution of business policy by tourist undertaking whether private or state owned at local, regional, national or international level to achieve the optimal satisfaction of the needs of identifiable consumer groups, and in doing so to achieve an appropriate return."

Product of Tourism

Tourism marketing and marketing in general both emphasise consumer orientation and satisfaction. The concept of consumer orientation, however, makes it necessary to understand the components of the tourist product from the point of view of the consumer. The product for the tourist covers the complete experience from the time he leaves home to the time he returns.

Availability of a product is the prerequisite in the marketing function. Unless there is a certain product, be it tangible or intangible or a service, marketing is not possible.

A product may be defined as the 'Sum of the physical and psychological satisfactions it provides to the buyer.' 'Marketing' by definition is the development of a product to meet the needs of the consumer and then employing the techniques of direct sales, publicity and advertising to bring this product to the consumer. In the case of tourism product, the basic raw materials would be the country's natural beauty, climate, history, culture and the people. Other aspects would be the existing facilities necessary for comfortable living such as water supply, electricity, roads, transport, communication and other essentials. In other words the tourist product can be seen as a composite product, as the sum-total of a country's tourist attractions, transport, accommodation and entertainment which hopefully result in consumer satisfaction. The tourist product can be entirely a manmade one or nature's creation improved upon by man. Each of these components of a tourist product is supplied by individual providers of services like hotel companies, airlines or other suppliers, and is offered directly to the tourists by them. A consumer can combine these individual tourist products through a large number of ways. There would be many possible destinations, each with a number of hotels, each to be reached by more than one airline.

Thus the potential choice facing the consumer is very large. A number of tourist destinations have placed at the disposal of a tourist a large variety of tourist products in abundant quantity from a large number of competing destinations. This, eventually, has led to the adoption of the new concept, i.e., the marketing concept in tourism by various countries promoting tourism. The important point about marketing is that it is applied to situations where the choice can be limited to a relatively small number of brands giving the consumer a reasonable choice. The process of selection thus becomes easier. In the field of tourism this process is taking place by the increasing use of 'package tours'. A package tour is a travel plan which includes most elements of vacation, such as transportation, accommodation, sight-seeing and entertainment. The tourist product is a composite product, whether it is sold as a package or assembled by the individual tourist himself or his travel agent.

Main Characteristics

Tourism, basically, is an infrastructure based service product. The nature of the service marketed being highly intangible and perishable offers a limited scope for creating and maintaining the distinctive competitive edge. Effective marketing of tourism needs constant gearing up of infrastructure to international standards and presupposes its coordination with the tourism suppliers. In strategic terms, it calls for the action of an integrated approach to management and marketing. In operational terms, it means the implementation of a better defined, better targeted market-driven strategy for realising the defined objectives.

Marketing of tourist product has certain peculiar characteristics. Although general principles of marketing of products of other industries could be applicable to marketing of tourist product, there are certain differences in approach. Among the peculiarities of the tourist product are:

Tourism is an Intangible, Non-material Product : No transfer of ownership of goods is involved as compared to a tangible product, say for example, a motor car. In tourism, instead, certain facilities, installations, items of equipment are made available for a specified time and for a specified use. For instance, a seat in an aeroplane or a train for a journey from one point to another or a booking in a hotel through a travel agent are carried out for a customer or services such as information and advice are provided.

Production and Consumption of Tourist Services are Closely Interrelated : The travel agent or tour operator who sells his product cannot store it. Production can only take place or can only be completed if the customer is actually present. There is a close link between production and consumption of tourist services. Most tourist services cannot be consumed incrementally. In other words, consumption, once begun, cannot be stopped, interrupted or modified at all. As a result, risk and uncertainty for the customer are higher, and his need for reliable pre-purchase information is stronger. The potential customer's decision-risk and dependence on accurate information is further increased because he cannot see, inspect, compare or try out tourist services before deciding to use them.

Multiplicity of Producers : The tourist product cannot be provided by a single enterprise. Each of the components of a tourist product is highly specialised and together make the final product. This is not so in the case of other tangible products where one manufacturer produces a total product. In tourism on the other hand, an airline considers 'seats flown' or passenger miles to be its product; a hotel produces 'guest nights' a travel agent 'bookings', a theatre and museum or an archaeological site measures its production' in number of visitors. In the tourist's view, however, the product he buys covers the complete experience of his visit to a particular place. In other words the tourist product is not an airline or a rail seat, or a hotel bed or a theatre ticket, but rather an amalgam of many components which together make a complete product. Because of these peculiar characteristics, coordination in marketing efforts, is very crucial.

Highly Unstable Demand : The demand is influenced by factors such as seasonal, economic, political, etc. The seasonal changes greatly affect the demand. Seasonality means that tourism plant is frequently used for a limited part of the year and therefore uneconomic. Many tourist areas have a short season - often as little as three months. A corollary of this seasonal usage is the seasonal unemployment, which is a serious problem. Some of the developing countries which have recently established tourist industries suffer particularly from seasonality. Seasonality also places strains on the transport system and other services. Thus seasonality presents a problem not only in relation to employment but also in relation to investment. On the other hand political unrest and economic instability caused by currency fluctuations and inflation, etc., greatly affect tourism demand.

Dominant Role of Intermediaries : In most industries, manufacturers have predominant control over product design; distribution and promotion and pricing. On the other hand in tourism, sales intermediaries like tour operators, travel agents, reservation services and hotel brokers play a very dominant role and enjoy superior marketing strength. From the standpoint of tourism marketing, this strong position of the travel trade has significant implications. The travel trade determines to a large extent which services will be sold and to whom. The type of services to be offered as well as the pricing policies and promotion strategies to be adopted by tourist enterprises, are, therefore, determined not only by the needs and preferences of the customers but also by those expressed by travel sales intermediaries.

Diverse Motivations : It is comparatively simple to determine why people buy a certain make of refrigerator, smoke certain brands of cigarettes, use certain brands of toothpaste or prefer a certain type of packaged food. The subjective and objective reasons, expectations and desires which influence tourists' choice for a certain holiday destination, type of accommodation and vacation activities are far less evident. Very often two people make exactly the same choices for entirely different and sometimes even mutually exclusive reasons. Travel motivations unlike motivations for buying a tangible article like a refrigerator, are heterogeneous - composed of diverse elements.

Marketing in tourism, due to the various factors mentioned above, as compared to marketing in other industries therefore needs a somewhat different approach.

Tourism marketing to a considerable extent depends on various market factors mentioned above. Unlike the normal consumer product or service, the tourist product is marketed at two levels.

1. The national or regional tourist organisation will be engage in a marketing campaign to persuade the potential tourist to visit the country or region for which it is responsible. In view of the fragmentation of supply, the complementarity of tourist services, the predominance of many small and medium sized enterprises and importance of tourism to an economy, the official tourist organisations have important functions in tourism marketing. The official tourist organisation will however not sell a tourist product directly to customers. It will have two major objectives. In the first place, it will seek to create knowledge of its country in tourist-generating markets and persuade visitors in these markets to visit that country. Secondly, it will seek to create an image of its country's tourist attractions in the best possible manner in tourist-generating markets so that the potential visitors are attracted
2. The various individual firms providing tourist services can market their own components of the total tourist product after the national tourist organisations have launched marketing campaigns to persuade the potential tourist to visit the country or region for which it is responsible.

Significant Activities

Marketing Function : It is basically customer-oriented, backed by integrated marketing aimed at customer satisfaction. The focus of marketing therefore centres around a customer. Professor Kotler in his definition has also emphasised this fact and stated that achievement of organisational goals depends on determining the needs of target markets (customers) and delivering the desired satisfaction more effectively and efficiently.

From the above it follows that organisations, before achieving their desired goals, have to go through series of marketing functions; and specific understanding of both marketing functions and specific marketing tasks becomes very crucial to grasp the subject of marketing. The marketing function can be considered as a system where interaction occurs between an organisation and a customer.

The main marketing functions and the tasks these functions set for themselves are as follows :

1. Market Research
2. Product formulation and development
3. Analysis and selection of target markets (segmentation)
4. Distribution networks
5. Product Promotion

Surveys and Research

Identifying the customer needs especially in a tourism industry which has very high service base content is very important. This is possible only through systematic market research and analysis. This is basic for successful marketing. It relates to providing answers to various questions pertaining to the marketing activities. Market research can be defined as the "Systematic collection of information relating to supply and demand for a product or a proposed product in such a way that the information may be used by the organisation to formulate informed decisions about its policies and its objectives."

The marketing process in fact starts by finding out answers to questions like who are the potential tourists, where do they come from, what axe their likes and dislikes, etc. In order to formulate any marketing strategy it is very essential for a national tourist organisation and others engaged in marketing a tourist product to know the answers to the following questions:

1. Who are the persons who engage in tourism and where do they live?
2. Who are the potential customers and where do they come from?
3. What are their likes and dislikes?
4. What are their travel preferences and interest?
5. What do they buy and where do they stay?
6. What mode of transport do they use?
7. What are their entertainment preferences?
8. What are the trends in competition?
9. What type of marketing programmes would be needed?

Answers to all the above questions are obtainable only through research. A tourist-organisation promotion effort, without appropriate answers to the above questions, will go waste. To make the overall marketing efforts effective and successful, the tourist organisation has to be totally aware of the trends in the travel habits, vacation habits and most important of all, the reasons attributed to the better success of a competing destination. A marketing manager cannot visualise successful marketing strategy without having an uptodate knowledge of their markets in general. It is very important to have detailed information on all the aspects of a market. Results of such research will work as guidelines for launching a successful marketing programme.

Different Methods

Market research is a continuous process. Among the variety of methods used, some seem to be widely resorted to because of their advantages over others. Research techniques can be grouped as:

1. Desk research
2. Field research
3. Sample surveys
4. Motivation research

Desk research includes the collection and analysis of all available data, statistics and published information on tourist trends and markets. In tourism much of the basic information about tourist trends and markets is available from existing sources. There are a number of international organisations like United Nations, WTO, EC, OECD, IATA, WTTC, ICAO, etc., which publish certain statistical information. Other data and statistics may be obtained from national tourist organisations, trade associations, carriers, hotel companies, etc. This information proves very useful in helping national tourist organisations to identify their markets and determine the objectives. This published information is of particular use to those countries which do not possess resources enough to undertake independent market research.

Field research, on the other hand, is the research work carried out in the tourist-generating markets itself. The special investigations in the field are to be carried out with a view to know more details of the market situation. Field research includes many methods among which the most common are the sample surveys and the motivation research.

Sample survey could be defined as the study of a given population through only a part or a fraction thereof. Much marketing information is obtained through the use of samples. In this method the population or 'Universe' for which information is required is defined, for example, all households in a country might be the universe or population under investigation. Then, a statistically valid sample of the population is drawn and information is obtained from the sample. Sampling techniques consist of personal interviews of tourists, travel agents, carriers and hotel managers, etc., by way of personal interviews with the help of prepared, questionnaires, by mailing questionnaires or through telephone contacts. There are certain advantages of this method. Lower cost is the major reason why data are collected by sampling in place of complete enumerations. The actual obtaining of information from the sample units (i.e., households in this case) is done by way of use of interviews and questionnaires. The questionnaire is administered to the sample population and various data obtained. The sampling place could be anywhere. Interviews may take place at homes or offices, at the place of arrival departure or temporary stay. In many countries there are a number of specialised firms which carry out sample survey enquiries, as well as government agencies similarly equipped.

The survey investigation can be classified by reference to the kind of information they seek to provide. There are surveys of market behaviour which record the holiday habits of the population, cross analysed by socio-economic, and other characteristics. The trends in holiday-making over many years may be seen and inferences made about the motives of holidaymakers. Furthermore, surveys may be undertaken to monitor the conduct of marketing campaigns.

Motivation research on the other hand attempts to describe and forecast the motives of the population under investigation, by use of techniques originally used in psychology. Assuming that every individual knows what he wants, motivation research is oriented to discover the needs of potential tourists in order to adopt the tourist supply accordingly and thus be able to satisfy them. In other words motivation research is the investigation into the motives behind travel. It concerns itself to answering the 'why' of human behaviour in contrast to answering the 'how' which is subject to sampling surveys. It analyses rather than describes the attitudes of both actual and potential tourists to travelling in general and to the tourist product offered in particular. Motivation research provides answers to very important questions. Research in the past has shown that people from some countries, are traditional good travellers (the French, the Germans, the American and the British), while others have become a nation of travellers only recently.

The most important techniques used in motivation research is the depth interview method. The questionnaire to be used for this method needs to be carefully designed, as motivation research aims at discovering the deep, subconscious and even unconscious of human beings. An ill-designed questionnaire is likely to reach no deeper than the conscious level where rational factors prevail. Other techniques used are the projective methods like word association tests, sentence completion test and pictorial tests, etc. and observations. Means have been devised to record the reactions of a person and to understand his motives.

Manufacture and Development

Having identified the consumers and the markets through the method of market research, the next step is the product formulation and development. The concept of consumer orientation makes it necessary to understand the various components of the tourist product from the point of view of the consumer. In the tourism industry product is what gives the consumer the various benefits they are seeking and its production and delivery. The formulation and development of a product involves factors like service, quality, range of different products offered in the market, the features and benefits it offers, and the brand name.

Availability of a 'product' is the prerequisite in the marketing function. Unless there is a certain 'product', be it tangible or intangible or a service, marketing is not possible.

A 'product' may be defined as the 'Sum of the physical and psychological satisfactions it provides to the buyer. 'Marketing' by definition is the development of a product to meet the needs of the consumer and then employing the techniques of direct sales, publicity and advertising to bring this product to the consumer.

In the case of tourism product, the basic raw materials would be the country's natural beauty climate, history, culture and the people. Other aspects would be the existing facilities necessary for comfortable living such as water supply, electricity, roads, transport, communication and other essentials. In other words the tourist product can be seen as a composite product, the sum-total of a country's tourist attractions, transport, accommodation and entertainment which hopefully result in consumer satisfaction. The tourist product can be entirely a manmade one or nature's creation improved upon by man. Each of these components of a tourist product is supplied by individual providers of services like retail travel agents, tour operators, hotel companies, airlines or other suppliers, and is offered directly to the tourist by them. A consumer can combine these individual tourist products through a large number of ways. There would be many possible destinations, each with a number of hotels, each to be reached by more than one airline. Thus the potential choice facing the consumer is very large. A number of enterprises have placed at the disposal of a tourist a large variety of tourist products in abundant quantity from a large number of competing destinations. This eventually has led to the adoption of the new concept, i.e., the marketing concept in tourism by various enterprises marketing tourism. The important point about marketing is that it applies to situations where the choice can be limited to a relatively small number of brands giving the consumer a reasonable choice. The process of selection thus becomes easier. In the field of tourism this process is taking place by the increasing use of package tours.

A package tour is a travel plan which includes most elements of vacation, such as transportation, accommodation, sight-seeing and entertainment. The tourist product is a composite product, whether it is sold as a package or assembled by the individual tourist himself or his travel agent. The tourist product can, therefore, be analysed in terms of; (i) Attractions; (ii) Facilities; (iii) Accessibility.

Tourist attraction is a very important element. Unless these are there, the tourists will not be motivated to go to a particular place. Attractions are those elements in the tourist product which determine the choice of a particular tourist to visit one particular destination rather than another. The attractions could be cultural like sites and areas of archaeological interest, historical buildings and monuments or scenic like flora and fauna, beach resorts, mountains, national parks or events like trade fairs, exhibitions, arts and music festivals, games, etc. Facilities are those elements in the tourist product which are a necessary aid to the tourist centre. *The facilities* complement the attractions. These include accommodations, various types of entertainments, picnic sites, recreation and so on. These are indeed important for every tourist centre. *Accessibility* is another important component in the tourist product. It is a means by which a tourist can reach the area where attractions are located. Tourist attractions of whatever type would be of little importance if their locations are inaccessible by the normal means of transport. If the tourist attractions are located at places where no means of transport can reach, or where there are inadequate transport facilities, these become of little value. The tourist attractions which are located near to the tourist-generating markets and are linked by a network of efficient transport, receive the maximum number of tourists.

Segmentation : Market segmentation is one of the important functions of marketing. The technique of market segmentation has been used by organisations to effectively target selected groups in the market with specially designed products and services. Market segmentation can be defined as "the process whereby producers organise their knowledge of current and potential customer groups and select for particular attention those whose needs and wants they are best able to supply with their products. According to Dibb, Simkin, Pride and Ferrell Market Segmentation is defined as :

"The process of dividing a total market into groups of people with relatively similar product needs, for the purpose of designing a marketing mix (or mixes) that precisely match the needs of individuals in a selected segment (or segments)."

From the above definition it emerges that the market segmentation is the process of identifying groups of buyers of a total market with different buying desires or requirements It identifies and analyses the socio-economic, life styles and motivational characteristics of potential buyers into useful categories and thereby launching advertising and promotional campaigns for these selected groups. The identification of segment of a total market is therefore of crucial importance. Due to manpower and financial constraints, it is not possible for an organisation to reach the entire market. Segmentation of the market in therefore made in order to achieve the most efficient use of marketing resources. The main objectives of the market segmentation, therefore, are :

1. Developing new markets for product variations or new products;
2. Developing defence against competitors by differentiating one's own product from theirs and matching it more closely to the requirements of a particular segment of the marker;
3. Achieving maximum effects for given expenditure on marketing activities, particularly communication activities;
4. Developing marketing programmes and budgets on the basis of a clearer idea of the response characteristic of specific segments.

The following information on the tourist markets will assists in segmentation :

1. Income distribution of overseas travellers and particularly correlations between income and distance travelled and travel expenditure;
2. Travel expenditure data, i.e., distribution of per head expenditure on travel;
3. Discretionary income of households, correlated with other characteristics enabling targets to be identified closely;
4. Historical trends in travel in different socio-economic categories;
5. Survey data on attitudes to and motivations for overseas travel;
6. Geographical dispersion of potential customers within the market;
7. Membership of clubs and associations associated with other characteristics which identify particular groups as potential customers;
8. Influence of intermediaries (travel agents, tour operators, wholesalers, carriers etc.) on destination choice in particular markets;
9. Relative importance of different intermediaries in particular markets (e.g., is all relevant type of travel business concentrated among relatively few intermediaries or it is dispersed throughout the market?).

The segmentation process divides the markets on the basis of several factors. The most important and commonly used market segmentation include the following:

1. Geographic segmentation
2. Demographic segmentation
3. Socio-economic segmentation

4. Psychological segmentation
5. Behavioural segmentation
6. Product-Based segmentation

Under each of the above principal variables, there are several areas which are considered while segmenting the travel markets. These are as follows:

Geographical : Operational areas, e.g., sales regions. Sales Districts such as provinces, cities, Political administrative zones.

Demographic : Age groups Sex differences Ethnic origin Marital status Religious affiliations.

Socio-economic : Income Levels Types of occupation Social class. Educational level of economic activity.

Psychological : Individual life-styles Personality types Perceptual differences Motivational differences.

Behavioural

Patterns of purchase.

Loyalty to fashions.

Levels of brand loyalty.

Benefits/recognition sought.

Product-based

Travel purposes.

Type of holiday.

Average length of stay.

Type of accommodation.

Mode of travel.

Arrangements for travel.

Individual / group travel.

In tourism, market segmentation is very important. The strategy of market segmentation in tourism recognises that a few vacation areas are universally acceptable and desired. Therefore, rather than waste promotional resources trying to please all travellers, the best market strategy is to isolate those segments of the entire market which are likely prospects and aim at the promotional efforts specifically to the needs of these selected groups. Thus, one of the early steps in marketing tourism is to divide the present and potential market on the basis of meaningful characteristics and then concentrate on promotion, supply and pricing efforts on serving these most prominent sections of the market - the target markets. Usually as stated earlier, the market segmentation for tourists is in terms of the following criteria: demographic, geographic, psychographic, social and economic.

For example, market for particular area might be largely archaeologists in their middle years who have an income of over $100,000 per year and who live in mid-eastern United States, or it might be largely businessmen in the age group of say 40-60 years who have an income of over $150,000 per year and who live in southern parts of West Germany. In tourism marketing, the total tourism market can be divided into the above major segments. A further segmentation, however, is possible within each of the above major segments for practical marketing purposes, and includes:

The Vacation Tourist : The vacation or the holiday tourist is the most common and popular tourist. He is immensely affected by changes in price, and is easily influenced by skilled and aggressive marketing effort. This type of tourist is resort-oriented (Rome, Bombay, New York, London, Paris are resorts as much as Venice, Goa, Pattaya, Miami). The vacation tourist market has been regarded as highly seasonal.

The Business Tourist : In recent years the market for this type of tourist has increased greatly. The choice of destination of a business tourist is generally determined by the nature of his business. The marketing efforts will not influence much the choice of the business tourist. As in the case of the vacation tourist who has proved to be very sensitive to price changes, the demand for business tourism is relatively price-inelastic. The demand will tend to be big-city oriented. The visits are of shorter duration and relatively frequent. The trade fairs, conventions, exhibitions, conferences and similar other events attract this kind of tourism.

The Common Interest Tourist : This segment comprises visits to relatives and friends, and visits for the purpose of education, for pilgrimages, etc. Demand for this type of tourism will be relatively price-elastic. The common interest tourist will not be easily influenced by the promotional efforts. The average length of stay of this type of tourist will be relatively longer. Because of his friends and relatives, he will not be a significant user of hotel and other such types of accommodation. The visits will not be frequent and expenditure relatively little on his stay as compared with other two groups.

Market segmentation in tourism has developed from the realisation that there is no such thing as a homogenous tourist market. Tourist market is composed of several homogenous sub groups having same wants, desires and behaviour etc. It is therefore advantageous for an organisation/company to serve one or more of these segments.

Marketing Segmentation

1. Delineation of the segment and identifying its potential.
2. Target market selection matching the characteristics of those segments with what you have to offer.
3. After matching the two, preparing a marketing plan or programme based on marketing mix.
4. Implementation and control or monitoring.

The Strategy

1. When the total market is diffused demographically, geographically and psychologically.
2. When the organisation has been in business for several year already.
3. When there are several competitors.
4. When most competitors employ a segmentation strategy.

It may however be mentioned here that the market segmentation in itself is not sufficient. The identification and location of potential buyers of a tourism product or service does not ensure that purchases will be effected. Market segmentation is merely the first initial step in the development of a total marketing strategy of a firm or an enterprise. It helps in the process of converting as many as possible of the potential buyers into actual buyers.

Market Mix

The most important objective of a tourist enterprise is to achieve the best results. This to a larger extent depends on a properly conceived marketing plan through which a strategy is to be developed to achieve the best results. Through the segmentation process appropriate targets are identified and analysed. The marketing strategy thus developed would now attempt to penetrate and persuade the target markets through a variety of tools mainly promotion and advertising. In addition, the marketing strategy will also look into the crucial question of pricing and distribution. The various tools are to be mixed in such a way that the enterprise obtains the optimal use of financial and manpower resources available at its disposal.

The mixture of various marketing tools is called the 'marketing mix'. Marketing mix is a mixture of elements which interact and complement each other to achieve targeted results. The term was first introduced by Professor Neil Bordes in the year 1953 when he got the cue from a study of Management of Marketing costs which described the marketing executive as a mixer of ingredients. Professor Philip Kotler, has defined the 'marketing mix' as the set of marketing tools that the firm uses to pursue its marketing objectives in the target market.

Tourist Marketing Mix : Tourist 'marketing mix' is largely a complex group of several factors intervening to achieve the marketing 'end product' which is increased effectiveness in demand output in relation to supply and marketing investment by tourist enterprises. Marketing mix helps the marketing manager of an enterprise whether individual or firm or an official tourism organisation to understand where marketing action can be initiated to improve the acceptability of a tourist product and stimulate the demand within the market. A tourist enterprise with a combination of specific activities can achieve the best possible results. It can decide *which* specific activity to use, *how* it is to be used, *when* and *where* to use and what resources to be allocated to them. A judicial mixture of activities at the appropriate time would give the enterprise to achieve its set marketing objectives.

The different components or elements of the mix may be seen as cooperating with or replacing each other as complements or substitutes. An example would be a policy of price reduction by an enterprise to tourist services or facilities which could be substituted by enhancing/ increasing available facilities and services for the same price or by strengthening various promotion activities in view of competition offered by competitors and thereby increasing the sales output. A strategy to combine both reduction of prices and at the same time offering extra facilities or extra advertising and promotion may or may not however always be efficient or result oriented. It is therefore essential that the target markets must be clearly defined for the success of marketing mix strategy.

Main Variables : Marketing mix incorporates four core variables. The four variables or four Ps as originally used to describe marketing mix by McCarthy in the year 1960 are :

1. Product
2. Price
3. Promotion
4. Place

Each of the above variables includes within it many sub-elements. Cowell in the year 1993 however revised the marketing mix variables for service industry including the travel and tourism. According to Cowell in addition to four original elements of product, price, promotion and place, there are three more which are :

1. People
2. Physical Evidence
3. Process (Customer involvement variables)

The three revised variables as introduced by Cowell in 1993 are to be used for travel and tourism since being a service industry it has certain special features. The use of marketing mix in travel and tourism has both short as well as long term aspects. The short term aspects relate to meeting the immediate initiatives of the competitors and include aspects like :

1. Price reduction
2. Aggressive promotion
3. Introduction of a new product
4. Special offers
5. Incentives

Long term aspects relate to meeting the objectives set aside for future long duration plans. These are based on longer range plans and are derived from the study of all kinds of trends in the market like natural, economic, social environmental and technological. The four variables or Ps have been illustrated below with illustrations taken from a well known and a branded tourist product. 'Palace on Wheels' is a famous train with historic charm and modern conveniences. For one week it is possible to roll back the pages of Indian History. The royal train takes the tourist on a royal Odyssey bringing alive the luxury of princely travel of the bygone age of the Raj. The train has been designed to offer all the modern comforts. The journey offers a complete package and covers nine well known historic cities in north India. Most of the travelling is done during night and the days are left free for discovering the various attractions.

Palace-an-Wheels

1. Various special features and characteristics of the product
2. Size and facilities offered
3. Service elements of the product
4. Benefits it offers
5. Image, reputation
6. Branding
7. Positioning - upmarket / down market

Price

1. Normal
2. Promotional
3. Corporate
4. Discounted
5. Wholesaler
6. Seasonal

Promotion

1. Advertising
2. Sales promotion
3. Press and public relations
4. Brochure / Folder
5. Personal selling
6. Direct mail
7. Outdoor
8. Sponsorship
9. Point-of-sale material

Place (Distribution)

1. Travel agents
2. Tour operators
3. Airlines
4. Reservation system
5. Direct from producers
6. Trade fairs and exhibitions
7. Clubs
8. General sales agents (GSA)

In the last century, the first fifty years made tourism a major worldwide industry. The emergence of the middle class in Europe along with the technological, political and social events of the day gave a great thrust to tourism. A large number of people were moving out both for leisure and business purposes. This period saw the mass movement of people annually from their home location to another country for a temporary stay for a few days or a week This mass movement of tourists was, however, predominant between Europe and America as the conditions of travel between the two continents were perfect. A fairly good infrastructure was already in existence. The necessary elements for travel like time, money and motivation were present. In addition to international movements there was also growth in domestic tourism. The invention of the motor car in Europe and USA, as also technological advancements in rail transport together with construction of networks of highways, gave a boost to domestic tourism.

Although the annual migration of people began rather more than a century ago, the present-day exodus especially in relation to international tourists is essentially a post-World War II phenomenon. The period between the two world wars can also be associated with the great movement of people for the purposes of tourism as a result of development of various modes of transport, especially the motor car and the aeroplane. The encouraging trend, however, received a setback as the Second World War intervened.

Tourism is sensitive to world economic and political conditions. It can occur on a large scale where the great majority of people enjoy some prosperity and security. Tourism and holidaymaking, on global as well as national scale, is a manifestation of prosperity and peace. As a great number of people in many countries have higher living standards, they can afford to set aside a proportion of their incomes for holidays and recreation.

Air travel blossomed during the post-World War II period resulting in rapid development of tourism. As the world began to settle down after the years of readjustments immediately after the War in 1945, there had been a rapid increase in both domestic and international tourism. The United Nations reported that in the ten-year period between 1955 and 1965, the number of tourist arrivals in some sixty-five countries increased three times from around 51 million to over 157 million. This, however, was only a beginning.

In the 1960s, USA, Germany, UK, France, Canada, Belgium, Luxembourg, The Netherlands, Italy, Switzerland,

Sweden, Denmark and Austria represented the twelve main tourist-generating countries. These twelve countries accounted for some three quarters of all international tourist arrivals in the world. The first two—USA and Germany—accounted for more than one-third of the world tourist arrivals. The reasons for this are very clear. These were the countries which enjoyed prosperity and higher standards of living, the two main factors conducive to growth of tourism. The development in the means of speedy transport and communication was also witnessed in these countries more significantly. This rapid increase in tourism in the above countries was therefore the outcome of such factors as prosperity and higher standards of living leading to increased leisure, improved education and, above all, the rapid strides they made in speedy transport and communication.

The trend in the growth of international tourism continues since the mid-1960s. The growth continues to be determined by the living standards in the developed countries. The widespread introduction of holidays with pay to a large majority of people is yet another important factor responsible for growth of tourist traffic.

In 1976, there were nearly 220 million international tourist arrivals in the world. This is an increase of more than 90 per cent over 1965. During 1965-1976, which was a period of intensive economic development in most industrialized countries, international tourism grew at an average rate of over 7 per cent annually. During this period, most of the developing countries were also able to benefit from the growing trend in the developed countries to consume tourist products. As mentioned elsewhere, tourism and its development are closely related to consumers' purchasing power and, in turn, to any domestic or international economic fluctuations. In the year 1974, the world economy was seriously affected by the energy crisis which occurred at the end of 1973. As a result, there was inflation which was responsible for the lower purchasing power. Tourism, like all other sectors of production and consumption, suffered the economic consequences of that crisis. The total international tourist arrivals in 1974 dropped by over two per cent in relation to 1973.

In the year 1975, as a result of efforts made by the governments of industrialised and developing countries to keep inflation within acceptable limits, there was resumption of production and consumption in the main generating countries. As a consequence, there was likewise a resumption of international travel. The total international tourist arrivals in 1975 amounted to roughly 213 million. The total number of international tourist arrivals in 1976 was estimated at between 218 and 222 million, which is a rise of between 2 and 4 per cent over 1975. According to the most recent estimates produced by the Secretariat General, World Tourism Organization, international tourist arrivals in 1999 were estimated to total 700 million, an increase of many folds over 1978.

Europe and North America continue to be the principal generating as well as receiving areas for international tourism, accounting for 70 per cent and 20 per cent respectively, of the international tourist arrivals. There is continuous trend of increase in international tourist arrivals in these areas since the year 1965. It may be stressed here that intra-regional tourism— tourism between countries of the same region—has an appreciable influence on the distribution of world arrivals. Thus, while domestic tourist movements tend to increase more and more, holidaymakers and tourists tend at the same time to travel farther from their usual place of residence, first in their own region and afterwards beyond it. Of the total international tourist movements within Europe and North America, at least 74 per cent are intra-regional. For Africa, it may be estimated that nearly 40 per cent of the tourist flows are intra-regional. In Americas, the United States and Canada alone account for nearly 50 per cent of all international tourist traffic in the region, where intra-regional international tourist movements are therefore predominant. In South Asia, intra-regional tourist movements may be estimated at between 20 and 30 per cent of the total tourist traffic in the region. In Europe, intra-regional tourism accounts for over 73 per cent of international tourist movements. However, a glance at the figures would indicate that most of the destinations are the same which were prominent in the year 1961. There is nevertheless a significant change in the number of arrivals in each of the destination. For instance, in 1961, France had generated 10.0 million tourists. This has been increased to almost 72 million in the year 1999. The big surprise, however, is China which received 27 million tourists in 1999.

The values are based upon preliminary data estimated for the full year supplied to World Tourism Organization (WTO) secretariat by the tourism authorities of the countries and territories concerned. Most countries and territories do not have the figures available for the whole year. However, experiences from the earlier years have shown that projections tend to be somewhat conservative. This implies that total figures might increase slightly when final figures are computed.

The most significant expansion of tourism has taken place primarly in the advanced industrialized countries, where tourism has become a part of life-style and consumption pattern of most people. Europe and Americas together account for almost 78 per cent of the total international tourist arrivals. The remaining 22 per cent is shared between East Asia/Pacific, Africa, Middle East and South Asia. South Asia's share is just one per cent of the total.

The Development

The basic causes of this rapid growth of demand for tourism in the highly developed industrialized countries in the course of the recent decades are economic, social and technological in nature. Rising per-capita incomes leading to higher purchasing power and an increase in discretionary incomes have made tourism accessible to a large majority of people. Today in advanced countries, a large majority of people can afford an annual holiday. In fact, many can even afford to take 'second holiday' of longer or shorter duration. In the case of more affluent members of the society, establishment of what may be called "recreation homes", e.g., seaside flatlets, country cottages, caravans, cruising boats, etc., have become a fashion and a status symbol. Secondly, more and diverse types of holiday and recreation are becoming popular. For example, in addition to comparatively recent developments such as holiday camps, caravans and coach tour, there are even newer fashions such as yachting, trail riding, safari and archaeological holiday. Increased mobility as a result of use of motor car for travel is another important economic factor which is responsible for growth in tourism in Europe and North America. Ownership of private motor cars in these areas grew tremendously resulting in more travel, including travel for the purpose of tourism.

CHAPTER–5

MOTIVATING FACTORS

There are many employee motivation factors that a manager must consider. In order to properly conduct business employees need to be well trained and motivated. How a manager goes about this task is extremely important.

One of the most important employee motivation factors is treating people fairly and with respect. As a manager if you do not respect your employees, you will never be able to motivate them. Furthermore, they will not respect you. You can show that you respect your employees by assigning them tasks that they are best suited for. Everyone one has a unique set of skills and talents. These skills and talents are a huge resource for a savvy manager. By accentuating your employees strong points you make them feel good, and they are motivated because they can accomplish tasks best suited for them.

Using these talents wisely leads us to another set of employee motivation factors. Managers need to develop the leaders around them. Building on an individual's strengths also allows them the motivation to work on areas they are not strong in. Correctly combining tasks for employees that focus on their strengths but also challenge them to do better in their weaker areas builds a great employee base. Now the employees are starting to take on more and more challenging projects with confidence. This leaves a manager to do what they need to do — manage. It also builds employee self esteem and confidence. A confident employee is one who is easily motivated. Also, by allowing them to develop into very productive individuals you are showing respect for their talents. This in and of itself is motivating. It starts a cycle of self motivation and confidence that continually builds upon its own momentum if carefully managed. This leads to a very strong and loyal employee base. Companies with this type of management get things done.

The best advice on employee motivation factors is to start a cycle of self confidence and motivation by developing each individual's strengths. This becomes a can-do situation for everyone. The really great thing about this is it builds positive energy within the company. Positive energy always breeds more positive energy. What better way to motivate employees than from within themselves!

Motivation in Tourism

According to the sociologist Max Weber, motivation lies at the core of human behaviour. Consequently, the study of motivation is central to any social scientific undertaking since it provides understanding, explanation and prediction. It goes beyond the how questions of description to the why questions of interpretation and causality. As one domain of interpersonal activity, tourism is no exception to this general observation. Indeed, 'why do people travel?' is probably the most fundamental issue in tourism research today.

However, given that tourism is also a many-faceted phenomenon requiring multidisciplinary treatment, clearly the answer provided to the vast and complex question of international movement (motivation as movement being derived from the Latin movere), will be predicated on the perspective of the analyst. Economists, for example, may emphasise the dynamics of consumer choice over competing pursuits and their effects on scarcity, price and profit.

Historians might wish to highlight the fact that patterns of travel go in periodic trends from the pleasure motives of Ancient Rome to the religious motives of the medieval pilgrimages and the educational motives of the Grand Tour. Geographers, environmentalists, political scientists and anthropologists will all have their own contributions to make to the mosaic of meaning underpinning reality. Each is a partial version of the truth. No single discipline can claim a comprehensive monopoly to the whole. Nevertheless, in tourism research, if there are two disciplines which perhaps stand out as having generated the greatest discussion on motivation, they are those of psychology and sociology.

At the risk of oversimplification, psychologists focus on the individual personality and intrinsic motivation, including cognitive and affective motives which are self-directing, autonomous and non-deterministic. Pearce's (1982) research is a good example of this position. Steering a middle course between psychoanalytic theories, which attempt to account for all spheres of human endeavour in terms of sexual and aggressive instincts, and those which exclude activities on the grounds that they are simply the result of habit and reflex, Pearce argues that this macro-perspective should be replaced with mini-theories which target specific groups and populations. Moreover, within this micro-framework, he maintains that a fruitful motivational paradigm for understanding tourism is one which combines self-actualisation with achievement and attribution theory. More specifically, Pearce contends that tourism research should address the future-oriented tasks of its subjects, be open to the possibility of multi-motives, examine the views of individual tourists rather than indulge in post hoc interpretative glosses of the researcher, and tackle the problems of empirical measurement. Drawing initially on Maslow's work, Pearce believes that the enhancement of self through tourism is the zenith of a hierarchy which requires progressive satisfaction from the basic physiological needs of hunger, shelter and so on, to those of safety, love, esteem and self-fulfilment. Later he develops these ideas in relation to a tourist career path which is based on stages of the life cycle.

By contrast, the sociological treatment of the tourist places the accent on society rather than on the individual, on extrinsic rather than on intrinsic motivation. Following the sociologist Emile Dur-kheim, Dann (1981) demonstrates that the prevailing conditions in the tourist's home environment are ultimately the dispositions for travel. Thus, the effects of an anomic existence (perceived normless-ness and meaninglessness), may act as motivational push factors that persuade people to seek temporary respite in another society which is deemed to be less fraught with such problems . Tourism provides the means for this escape. Similarly, persons who suffer from lack of belonging in their own society, chiefly through denial of status advancement, may journey to those parts of the world (often developing countries) where they are treated with greater respect. It is further possible to design a continuum ranging from predominantly anomic to ego-enhancement motives, and to identify social profiles of toursits which, to a greater or lesser extent, measure up to these ideal typical constructs.

An extension of the sociological framework is provided by Sharpley (1994). He points out that there are several concrete social influences conditioning the decision to travel. He identifies the family, reference groups, social class, the surrounding culture and the workplace as the most important of these. The latter is particularly significant since it is conducive to compensatory and spillover effects in various types of travel. Thus, boring or monotonous jobs may lead to the quest for excitement, stress may result in a search for relaxation, and the regimentation of the office or factory may encourage the pursuit of ludic activities elsewhere. Alternatively, type of occupation, especially if self-rewarding, may stimulate similar interests on a vacation (such as the history teacher travelling to an archaeological site). As far as the influence of home culture is concerned, Parrinello (1993), in a postmodern context, has noted the tremendous impact of consumerism and product advertising on the decision to travel. For her, citizens of most developed countries live in a tourism-saturated environment and are daily bombarded with images of abroad.

Whereas at first glance psychological and sociological approaches may appear diametrically opposed, in many respects, they can be regarded as complementary. Whether one begins or ends with the individual or society, essentially both are intertwined. Indeed, if points of convergence rather than differences are stressed, several worthwhile advances in tourism motivational research can be identified. The first sign of mutual progress is a shared concern for theoretical awareness. Even though there are intra-paradigmatic differences attributable to schools or perspectives within each discipline, some sort of working consensus can be achieved with respect to terminology. In this regard, operational definitions can be agreed upon as to what exactly constitutes motivation, and how this varies from the allied concepts of aspiration, intention, reason, purpose, satisfaction, aim and goal. Thus, most psychologists and sociologists would concur that when tourists are asked to complete embarkation forms by stating the purpose of their trip in terms of business, pleasure or visiting friends and relatives, these categories, although possibly useful to the compilers of statistics, do not represent the full motivational meaning of a trip. Similarly, they would agree that many surveys which measure differences between expectation and reality are in fact dealing with satisfaction rather than motivation.

Another realm of theoretical convergence is the appreciation that motives, while reasonable to one individual, may be far from rational or logical to another. Hence, a person who, quite reasonably to himself or herself, seeks self-identity through the rigours of wilderness travel may be considered quite irrational by those who wish no more than relaxation by the hotel swimming pool. Furthermore, both may be regarded as distinctly odd by members of a destination community. What is meaningful and reasonable for one person may be motivationally senseless for another, especially when the other is a researcher. The important point is to realise how situations are defined, and then seek to monitor rather than to judge them.

A further area of theoretical consensus resides in the common belief that tourist motivation is future-oriented. From the psychologist's point of view, the experience should be seen in the context of long-term goals. From the sociologist's standpoint, Alfred Schutz's 'in-order-to' motivation is regarded as imaginatively projected action: as if it had already taken place as part of a meaningful project. That is why the verbal and pictorial discourse of tourism advertising is frequently couched in the future perfect tense, and why anticipation of a holiday is so important.

At the methodological level, both psychologists and sociologists emphasise the significance of an emic perspective. Pearce, for instance, has shown that personal accounts of negative and positive tourism experiences can reveal inferable motives, whereas the checklist approach of the structured survey only indicates superficial agreement with the a priori motivational categories that the investigator feels are worthy of inclusion. Many sociologists agree, to the extent that recent motivational research has employed projective tests whereby subjects linguistically frame their own responses to destination images.

Methodologically, too, psychologists and sociologists both appreciate that tourists may be unwilling, or even unable, to articulate their real motives for travel. Shared realisation of this difficulty has prompted such innovative research strategies as 'systematic lurking' and 'conversation sampling', which focus on the rarely investigated but nonetheless highly germane factor of word of mouth communication at all stages of a trip, including the ever more salient domain of pre-trip anticipation. Such techniques can be particularly useful in tapping the increasingly evident nostalgia motivation in contemporary tourism, one that is correspondingly difficult to unearth through the traditional methods of interviewing and questionnaire completion.

Finally, psychologists and sociologists agree that tourist motivation, like all motivation, is a highly subjective issue. The problem thus becomes how to study the realm of the subjective in an objective or dispassionate manner. For some (including con-structivists and critical theorists), this is a non-issue, since value freedom in research is neither possible nor desirable. For others, subjectivity is explored not in its individuality but in its typicality. According to this view, one is not so much concerned about why John Doe goes on holiday as to why the type of person John Doe represents decides to take a vacation. Such a realisation has led to several typologies in tourism research, and these certainly constitute a useful starting point in understanding the tourist. However, typologies in themselves are heuristic, rather than explanatory, devices and more still remains to be done at both the theoretical and methodological level if the basic question of why tourists travel is to be adequately answered.

Motivation is the process by which people seek to achieve certain goals, which in turn satisfy a need. The word motivation is used to describe the things that motivate people, the process through which a goal satisfies a need, and the social process by which a manager seeks to influence the performance of a subordinate to increase productivity. Motivation is a key aspect of hospitality management and one of the mechanisms for tackling the high levels of labor turnover within the industry in developed countries. The academic discussion of motivation has been dominated by a dichotomy between the study of the things that motivate – content theories – and the process by which people are motivated – process theories. Content theories of motivation focus on identifying the things or situations to which employees aspire as a way of describing motivation. Generally, they explain that people are driven to fulfill needs that are deficient or unsatisfied such as a desire for more money, promotion, responsibility or personal fulfillment.

Therefore to motivate someone one must first identify their individual level of need. Content theorists believe that such needs are innate in humans. The main examples of Content theories are Maslow's Hierarchy of Needs (1943) and Herzberg's Two Factor Theory (Herzberg et al., 1959). Herzberg differentiated between the things that would prevent dissatisfaction and the things that would motivate employees. The 'dissatisfiers' tended to be extrinsic rewards or outcomes, benefits provided by the organization such as pay increases, working conditions, and interpersonal relations. It was recognized that extrinsic rewards are less effective as motivators, except in the short-term. The 'motivators' tended to be intrinsic rewards, outcomes or benefits that come from within the individual themselves, such as feelings of satisfaction, self-esteem, feelings of achievement and competence or a sense of purpose and therefore the focus of motivational effort for managers should be on providing opportunities for responsibility, autonomy, personal development, and recognition.

However, such studies have been criticized for being ethnocentric; there is an assumption that the priorities associated with different levels of need are universal, whereas there is evidence to suggest that not only are levels perceived as more or less important depending on cultural values, but some levels do not exist at all (Yu, 1999). Also, the intangible nature of the 'product' in hospitality sometimes makes it difficult to measure the performance of an employee, so the process of recognizing and rewarding employees becomes more complicated.

Process theories of motivation seek to explain the reason why people might be motivated and the individual differences evident in people's choices of goals and behaviors, rather than identifying the things that are motivators. Examples are theories such as equity theory, expectancy theory, and goal-setting theory, all of which seek to describe the cognitive processes that people follow in evaluating motivational drives. Expectancy theory (Vroom, 1964), for example, explains the process by which someone is motivated as a product of the relationship between the effort that they have to expend and the likelihood that their effort will lead to a reward that they value. For example, although people are not solely motivated by money, if a waiter recognizes that better service might lead to a bigger gratuity for them personally, they may be motivated to increase their service level. However, this situation might not be as motivating if tips are pooled and therefore the increase in their share would not be significant enough to merit extra effort as the value of the final reward is either too small or not directly related to the amount of effort (if other waiters give poor service and subsequently contribute little to pooled tips). Process theories have been criticized for being overly intellectualized; however, they do provide alternative practical insights into the motivation debate. Some methods of increasing employee motivation have centered on redesigning the jobs and tasks that people do. Job rotation redesigns work by switching employees from task to task at regular intervals. This can be an attempt to relieve the boredom of low-skilled tasks, as it provides some variety in the tasks undertaken, to share responsibility for unpopular tasks or as part of a training program. For example, employees may be rotated through reception duties, bar work, restaurant work or kitchen duties, either as a way of covering for staff shortages or training on new skills. Although this increases flexibility for the organization, it does not enrich the job for the jobholder, as skills are all at a similar level and individual tasks remain the same.

Job enlargement redesigns jobs by combining a number of tasks at a similar skill level to increase the length/scope of the job. Although this can reduce boredom and increase interest in work, it does require greater knowledge, skill, and training. For example, rather than have waiters for each course or drinks order in a restaurant, they could be given responsibility for the complete ordering of a small number of tables. This would increase the length of time they are involved in their task. However, it does not necessarily make the component parts of the job any more interesting or rewarding.

Job enrichment, based on the work of Herzberg outlined above, seeks to increase the level of satisfaction of workers by addressing the factors that motivate individuals and including these in the redesigned role. Instead of increasing the job horizontally, as happens with job enlargement, the job is increased vertically, by increasing the employee's responsibility and autonomy by adding elements such as planning, organizing, and control. For example, levels of supervision can be decreased to give workers more control and responsibility over their workload, work pace, and quality of output. They can also be encouraged to take on more direct customer interaction or responsibility for a larger part of the process. An alternative classification of motivation theories focuses on whether they are 'near to' tasks undertaken in the workplace (proximal) or at some 'distance' from it (distal). Evidence so far suggests that proximal theories such as goal setting are more powerful at motivating employees than their distal counterparts.

Factor

Our true motivations come from deep inside our subconscious, from our inner values. Our values represent what is important to us. They dictate how we spend our time, how we live our life and give us a scale of how to judge what is right or wrong according to our experiences. We believe that our values are THE right ones and that others will have the same ones and act accordingly and if they don't then they are wrong.

Our values come from our family, society, school, the media, religion and the internet and as no two people will ever have had the same life there are no two sets of values the same. It is from our values that we get our motivation. Put it this way, if you place no real value on an aim or goal, you will have no motivation to achieve it.

What we tend to do is to manage people according to our own motivation. Culturally we are accustomed to being told what to do, starting with our parents, school and then our bosses until we are in a position where we are managing others. At each level the person telling us what to do is using what they feel is important. Our parents base their advice on their generation's values and history and our teachers are driven by exam results and test scores.

When we get into the work place quite often it is our first boss who then influences us about what is important in business and where to place our emphasis and energy. We in turn continue this cycle and create another generation of managers who dictate to staff, believing that what motivates them will motivate their staff and again miss that fact that we are all unique and will therefore have a unique way of being motivated.

There are two ways to be motivated; towards something or away from something. When managing others we use the carrot or the stick. Traditionally when we tell someone what to do there is either an implied, or a very real threat of the consequences should they not comply with what we have asked for and the other way of course is to promise financial rewards or a promotion.

If you think of the towards/away from motivation as two ends of a continuum, most peoples' management techniques are somewhere along that line using a combination of carrot and stick.

However , the result of this is limited as it is based on what we think is motivating for us and is ultimately ineffective in terms of getting the most out of your staff.

There is another way.... Inner motivation. If you can find out what it is that really motivates someone internally to perform to their full potential and communicate with them in their language ,what you will find is that there is little need to manage that person in the traditional meaning of the word. In traditional management the boss dictates, persuades, debates and cajoles his staff to get the results he wants.

It is quick and easy and provides the manager with a feeling of being in control. By motivating a person internally, what you are doing is going beyond the carrot and stick and providing for that person the basis for them to take full responsibility for their performance. When internally motivated a person will not need to be held by the hand every step of the way, problems will be addressed immediately and the person will take responsibility for their own development as they will want to do the best they can.

Responsibility is a word that is paid great lip service but is seldom understood. In today's 'blame' culture it is all too easy to point the finger at another when things go wrong or not according to plan. Taking responsibility means to truly understand how our choices affect our lives and what affect those choices have on others around us. Responsibility allows us to create greater self esteem. Greater self esteem will reduce stress and generate higher performance, meaning that a win/win situation is then achieved.

So how do you internally motivate someone? The first step is to really want to create new culture in the organisation going from secrecy, hierarchy and censorship to one of openness, support and honesty. Then you have to believe that everyone is different and will have a different set of motivating factors that are unique and should be respected.

After that it is vital to improve communication skills. This includes listening skills, non-verbal communication and questioning techniques that enable the manager to be more of a coach than dictator and develop an understanding of how to help your staff achieve their best. Although a change in culture takes time, a factor many people use in order to avoid change, the outcome means less management time will be required in the future but the result will show in greater performance.

The over all benefits inner motivated staff will be; improved performance and productivity, improved relationships, more time for the managers, better use of people, skills and resources and greater flexibility and adaptability to change. In the age where the only certainty is change this has got to be the best way to stay ahead of the game, and enjoy life at the same time!

CHAPTER–6

THE DIFFICULTIES

Geneva, Switzerland–Switzerland, Austria and Germany have the most attractive environments for developing the travel and tourism industry, according to the third annual Travel & Tourism Competitiveness Report, released today by the World Economic Forum. France, Canada, Spain, Sweden, the United States, Australia and Singapore complete the top ten. This year's report, published under the theme of "Managing in a Time of Turbulence", reflects the many difficulties the industry currently faces, which must be overcome to ensure strong sectoral growth in the future. This is particularly captured by the topics covered in the analytical chapters, exploring issues such as the impact of oil prices on the tourism industry, the importance of price competitiveness for attracting tourists, and the extent to which the TTCI explains differences in travel intensity between countries.

"Our study aims to measure the factors that make it attractive to develop the travel and tourism industry of individual countries. The top rankings of Switzerland, Austria, Germany, France and Canada demonstrate the importance of supportive business and regulatory frameworks, coupled with world-class transport and tourism infrastructure, and a focus on nurturing human and natural resources for fostering an environment that is attractive for developing the travel and tourism sector," said Jennifer Blanke, Senior Economist of the World Economic Forum's Global Competitiveness Network.

This cross-country analysis of the drivers of competitiveness in travel and tourism provides useful comparative information to make business decisions and to add value to governments wishing to improve their travel and tourism environments. The rankings are based on the Travel & Tourism Competitiveness Index (TTCI) covering 133 countries around the world. The TTCI uses a combination of data from publicly available sources, international travel and tourism institutions and experts, as well as the results of the Executive Opinion Survey, a comprehensive annual survey conducted by the World Economic Forum, together with its network of Partner Institutes (leading research institutes and business organizations) in the countries covered by the report. The survey provides unique data on many qualitative institutional and business environment issues.

The last part of the report contains detailed country profiles for the 133 economies featured in the study, providing a comprehensive summary of their overall position in the Index rankings, as well as a guide to the most prominent travel and tourism competitive advantages and disadvantages of each. Also included is an extensive section of data tables covering each indicator used in the Index's computation.

"To thrive, or even survive, in this period of uncertainty and change, both the travel and tourism industry, and destinations themselves will need to approach the challenges in a holistic and systemic manner. This would allow innovative ideas to emerge, new directions to be taken, new alliances to be forged and profits to be reaped. This comprehensive approach to travel and tourism competitiveness taken in the report aims to contribute to this discussion," said Thea Chiesa, Head of Aviation, Travel and Tourism at the World Economic Forum.

"For the past four years, the World Economic Forum has engaged key industry and thought leaders through its Aviation, Travel & Tourism Industry Partnership Programme to carry out an in-depth analysis of the travel & tourism (T&T) competitiveness of economies around the world. The goal is to construct a platform for multistakeholder dialogue to ensure the development of strong and sustainable national travel and tourism industries capable of contributing effectively to international economic development," noted Klaus Schwab, Founder and Executive Chairman of the World Economic Forum.

"This Index will help governments and the industry identify areas where support in the sector can show big gains in the response to both the recession and climate change. Tourism competitiveness is a major element to be included in economic stimulation packages and the Green New Deal. Tourism is one of the largest employers in most countries and a fast-entry vehicle into the workforce for young people and women. Encouraging travel boosts consumer and business confidence. It strengthens two-way trade and it promotes export income – particularly for the poorest countries," said Geoffrey Lipman, Assistant Secretary-General, World Tourism Organization (UNWTO), Madrid.

"The economic downturn forces a new view on a country's T&T policy by the local government and the T&T industry to preserve the competitiveness of its destination. Competition between destinations will heat up, as many customers will manage their travel budget more tightly for some time. Moreover, a fast-growing number of customers have started making "green travel" part of their buying decision. And new climate change regulation ETS) will put additional costs-schemes (e.g. emissions trading scheme on destinations that underinvest in a sustainable and climate neutral T&T infrastructure. The local tourism players have to address both trends in parallel: on the one hand attracting increasingly budget sensitive customers by a superior marketing and sales initiative in the short term, and rethinking their T&T investment priorities under the emerging new paradigm of sustainable travel and tourism on the other" said Jürgen Ringbeck, Partner and Senior Vice-President, Booz & Company, Germany.

"Competitiveness is built with efficiencies across the entire travel and tourism value chain. This study highlights the benchmarks of best practice that will determine winning destinations. Luring an airline to start or increase transport links is critical in developing tourism markets. But long-term success can only be built with coordinated government policies. As governments battle the economic crisis and build a more solid future for their economies, ensuring a solid platform with effective policy for aviation and tourism growth must be a priority" said Giovanni Bisignani, Chief Executive Officer and Director-General of the International Air Transport Association.

"In these turbulent times the tourism and travel sector must not only focus on addressing immediate challenges but also longer term sustainability. Adaptability, deeper domestic tourism supply chains, 'quality and skill' investments, and diversity are of real importance and characteristics clearly evident in the T&T Competitiveness Index,' said Alex Kyriakidis, Managing Partner, Global Travel, Tourism and Leisure, Deloitte, United Kingdom.

"Although there are many uncertainties as to how long the current crisis will continue, and how deep its impact will be, past experience has shown that travel and tourism always rebounds from cyclical sometimes even stronger," said Ufi Ibrahim, Chief Operating-downturns Officer of the World Travel & Tourism Council (WTTC).

"Many economic stimulus packages are currently focusing on infrastructure development. The TTCI demonstrates the importance of infrastructure provision for tourism competitiveness. It's time for industry and governments to work jointly together to consider the implications for tourism in infrastructure planning" said Larry Dwyer, Qantas Professor of Travel and Tourism Economics, Australian School of Business, University of New South Wales.

The World Economic Forum produced the report in close collaboration with its Strategic Design Partner, Booz & Company, and its Data Partners, which included Deloitte, the International Air Transport Association (IATA), the International Union for Conservation of Nature (IUCN), the World Tourism Organization (UNWTO) and the World Travel & Tourism Council (WTTC). The Forum also received important feedback from a number of its key Industry Partners in the effort, namely Airbus, Abercrombie & Kent, Bombardier, British Airways, Carlson, Etihad Airways, Emirates Group, Hertz, Jet Airways, NetJets, Silversea, Swiss International Airlines and Rolls-Royce. Several thought leaders from these organizations also contributed insightful papers addressing various aspects of sustainable travel and tourism competitiveness. The World Economic Forum is an independent international organization committed to improving the state of the world by engaging leaders in partnerships to shape global, regional and industry agendas.

The Problem of Forecasting and Predicting Growth and Change

A feature of this text has been the forecasts about tourism's future. Witt and Song are clear about which methods work, and Frechtling (also in this volume) makes some telling points about which factors will influence tourism in the next decade. But most econometric and statistical trend projections are based on the principle of ceteris paribus – all things remaining equal. What if they do not? A feature of the 20th century, especially the second half of the century, was relative stability in many aspects of tourism, but this may not be true for the 21st century.

Global tourism is forecast to grow, but overall growth forecasts hide tremendous differences between regions and countries. According to Teye (this volume) Africa receives only 4% of all international tourists and only 2% of total international tourism receipts. He shows that many African countries are economically worse off now than they were 40 years ago, still over-reliant on agricultural and/or mineral production, with tourism presenting both cultural and environmental challenges. He concludes that there have been and still are a myriad of obstacles to tourism development, such as political instability, economic restructuring, human resource constraints, lack of regional co-operation and a lack of basic infrastructure.

An optimistic view of Europe and North America is that at best their tourism industries are stable. In their respective chapters, Cook states that short-term growth in US arrivals will be slow, whilst Cleverdon suggests tourism in Europe is growing at a rate of 3% compared with a global rate of 4%, and its market share is forecast to decline from 59% (1995) to 47% by 2020. On the other hand South America looks set for a period of sustained tourism growth. Arrivals have been growing at an annual rate of 9% and receipts at 12%. It has some tremendous advantages, including its relative proximity to lucrative North American markets, historic and language links with Europe, and excellent natural resources (rainforest/Andes/beaches).

Asia Pacific also seems to be on an upturn. Chamberlain (this volume) quotes the WTO as forecasting that this region will 'grow faster than any other' and will pass the Americas to become second to Europe in the number of visitor arrivals. This means five times as many visitors in 2020 as in 1998 – admittedly a low year – although there may be some difficulty in accommodating that number of visitors and it might pose strains on the infrastructure in the region. Asia Pacific illustrates perfectly how vulnerable these industries are to unexpected events. The recent financial crisis in this region led to dramatic falls in arrivals, hotel rates and hotel occupancies, not only in the Pacific region but globally . This kind of event makes forecasting tourism performance in some regions almost impossible. No one can predict what might happen in the Middle East, the Indian sub-continent and the Russian Federation. Political instability, economic turbulence and religious differences could all have negative effects on potential tourism development and growth.

Overall there is evidence of extremely rapid growth in some regions, that this growth will continue, and that other regions will begin to attain a greater share of tourism in the years ahead. But there is really no such thing as a 'fair share' despite what ministers and NTOs say. Not everywhere needs or can expect to attract large numbers of tourists. Those places that have not grown significantly or do not have major tourism industries generally are in that position for good reasons. Cetron (this volume) identified some of these reasons – a lack of perceived attractions compared to other areas, relative or absolute inaccessibility, unsuitable climate, political regimes which discourage tourism, problems of security, health and safety, relatively high cost and often a combination of several of these.

What is needed is an examination of which, if any, of these elements are likely to change significantly in the short- to medium-term future, to understand if those regions are likely to see major increases in tourism. Even then, should such a change in situation come about, we need to see whether the region is appropriately equipped to handle such an increase effectively. Rapid percentage growth is rather easy from a low base, but long-term sustained growth is what is important, if indeed it is growth that is desired. If the world is serious about sustainable development and living within the limits of the resources available, then growth, especially rapid growth, may not be the pattern desired or acceptable in all regions. This aspect is rarely tackled in forecasts, where the focus is normally on growth.

The Problem of Industry Characteristics

It seems clear there is going to be continued growth of global brands such as McDonalds and Burger King, Hilton and Holiday Inn, British Airways,One World Alliance, Thomas Cook and American Express, Avis and Hertz. Despite the fact that the Internet makes some people suggest the brand isdead, big firms will continue. There are still economies of scale to be achieved by being big, even in a world of e-commerce, as the AOL–Time Warner merger demonstrates. But the industries will continue to have many small operators managing unique operations on a local basis. One of the comments frequently made about tourism is its fragmentation and the difficulty this poses for instituting controls, particularly self-regulation by the industry. It often results in multiple, sometimes opposing, objectives among different players, which require different solutions in different locations. This is one of the reasons for the frequent lack of application and success of national master plans. Despite the globalization trends to which Chamberlain and others refer in this volume, there is likely to remain a large element of the tourism industry made up of very small players. The web should encourage and assist the maintenance of some of this diversity.

The tourism workforce is typically described as having low ability and few skills. Large numbers of young people are employed in these industries, expected to work long, unsociable hours, paid below average wages resulting in extremely high levels of staff turnover. This pattern may not be able to continue, if only because in many countries in the developed world there will be fewer young people to be employed under these or any conditions because of changing demographics. Changes in the composition of populations, nationally and globally, are likely to have major, if still uncertain effects on all aspects of tourism and hospitality in the coming century.

The Problem of Climate Change

A key problem that tourism and hospitality has to face is climate change. This issue could have greater effects on tomorrow's world and tourism and hospitality in particular than anything else discussed so far. Two islands have disappeared already because of rising sea levels, and the effects of El Nino and weather instability throughout the world have been terrible in recent years. The most worrying aspect is that very little is known about the full nature or level of these effects. To all intents and purposes the tourism and hospitality industries appear to have buried their heads in the sand and seem intent on ignoring what could be the major problem of the century.

Some of the likely effects as well as rising sea levels, include negative effects on ski areas with fewer days of snow-cover, increased cloud and rainfall in some areas, and increased temperatures and greater sun exposure in other parts of the world, with general increased turbulence and unpredictability of weather. Lohmann (this volume) showed that many of these are serious enough to at least threaten, if not change, the patterns of tourism and to have significant impacts on hospitality operations. If sea levels do rise significantly as forecast, many world cities including London, Tokyo, Los Angeles, Washington, Sydney and Singapore would be under water, as well as Bangladesh, the Maldives, the Seychelles, the Netherlands and Florida among others. There would be economic, political and social turmoil. Tourism depends on global economic well-being and this would not exist if this scenario became reality.

At this time, however, it seems that only the insurance and banking industries have begun to take real notice of what is likely to be a significant problem, not just for our industries but the world as a whole. Even if serious steps are taken to reduce the problem, it will be decades before the process is reversed, if indeed, it can be reversed. It is worrying that in general the problem is being ignored by forecasters and by planners. It seems rather naive, for example, to produce a tourism master plan for a place that might be under water by the time the plan is ready to be implemented.

Vietnam's Tourism Sector Faces More Difficulties

While many other industries are showing signals of recovery, the bad luck sector seems to accompany the tourism sector as the A/H1N1 epidemic is still spreading. The number of international arrivals to Vietnam continues to fall sharply. In May and June of 2009, the number of tourists from Vietnam's major markets was reduced by 70 percent. Over the past years, the number of international visitors from Asian nations accounted for an important market share of the country's tourism. South Korea, Japan, China, Malaysia, Singapore and Taiwan are among Vietnam's top ten markets for tourists.

However, only within two months, the A/H1N1 pandemic has seriously affected the tourism sector. Many key Asian markets have also experienced sharp fall. Particularly, the number of Japanese visitors to Vietnam through tourism companies has decreased by 70 per cent compared to the same period last year. The tourism companies which focus on Japanese visitors are nervous because they must cancel tours registered two or three months ago. Currently, tourism companies cannot estimate how many visitors they will welcome in July. This is not something good because Japanese are often in the habit of booking tours that last from two to three months or at least one month.

Ms My, a guide for Japanese tourists of a tourism company said she set up timetables to lead inbound tours to

Ho Chi Minh City and neighbouring localities every day. However, during these days, she received only one Japanese delegation every two weeks. My now is forced to guide outbound tours from Vietnam to Japan.

Being less difficult than the Japanese market, the number of visitors from other markets also reduced around 20 per cent-30 per cent on average. Big and luxury hotels in Ho Chi Minh City are also facing a difficult time as hotel room occupancy currently accounts for 56 per cent on average. Particularly, four to five-star hotels are running at a 40 per cent-50 per cent occupancy rate, falling 40 per cent compared to the same period of last year. The occupancy percentage may continue to fall further because of low tourism season. The price of luxury rooms at certain four to five-star hotels in Ho Chi Minh City has reduced by 40 per cent-50 per cent against that of last year. In front of the current difficulties, the country's tourism sector will have a hard time reaching the goal of 4.5 million international arrivals this year. It is forecast to welcome only around 3.2 million foreign visitors, down 20 per cent against the figure of 2008.

According to the latest survey results on Vietnam's hotel business in 2008 conducted by the Grant Thornton Vietnam, the occupancy rates of luxury rooms was lowest during the four past years. Although Vietnam's tourism sector has gained significant achievements in growing and luring international tourists and being listed among Asian-Pacific nations having a high growth, it has been attached with weaknesses Facilities and luxury rooms have not yet met the increasing demand, resulting in the increase in room prices. The price hike has caused a break between travel firms and hotels for many years. Sometimes, the price of luxury rooms is 30 per cent-40 per cent higher than other regional nations.

Recently, the United Nations World Tourism Organization (UNWTO) has predicted that the non-smoking industry, which contributes nearly 10 percent in GDP of the global economy, will overcome the negative impacts from the global economic downturn in 2010. It also forecasts that the number of tourists in the whole world will increase from 900 million to over 1 billion people in 2010 and may reach approx 1.6 billion in 2020. The recovery will be most obvious in the Asia-Pacific region, where the tourism sector represents a most rapid growth in the world thanks to the appearance of a new middle class. It is hoped that along with more investment poured into luxury hotels in Ho Chi Minh City, tourism businesses will have to adopt a sustainable strategy in order to prepare for the sector's foreseen recovery in the next one or two years.

CHAPTER–7

THE NETWORK

The Tourism Network team is les by Susan Briggs, working with Mary Tebje and Elias Moubayed. You're guaranteed sensible advice that you'll be able to implement straight away to increase profits, visitor spend and numbers. We've had "proper jobs" working directly for hotels, visitor attractions, e-commerce companies and destinations so have real and direct tourism industry experience. We focus only on projects we believe in and enjoy so we can really throw our energy and enthusiasm into finding and creating new markets and ways of working for our clients. Here are some of the tourism industry services that could benefit your business or area:

Tourism Marketing: Need to stand out from the competition and generate better profits or higher visitor numbers? Let us develop an action-oriented marketing plan for you or undertake specific aspects of marketing for you. This could include anything from writing press releases or improving your search engine rankings to undertaking a major campaign on your behalf. We've undertaken marketing for many tourism businesses and destinations over the last 20 years but pride ourselves on still coming up with new ideas and ways to stretch small marketing budgets even further.

Training: Would you like to improve your marketing skills, or just get some fresh input to your marketing? We develop and deliver practical and fun training sessions and marketing master classes. These include half day, full day and residential workshops as well as toolkits, virtual online classes and how-to publications. Participants leave our events full of ideas and advice they can implement immediately.

Facilitating Meetings and Events: Clients often ask us to facilitate board or partnership meetings, finding our independent advice invaluable. We help to increase collaboration, bring together diverse "factions", generate new opportunities and work through tricky problems. We also organise larger scale events such as tourism marketing conferences, either independently or on behalf of clients such as VisitBritain.

Writing and Publishing: Our writing and publishing services range from developing copy for brochures and websites to writing business support toolkits and books. Susan Briggs is author of numerous successful tourism industry publications. We develop "Tourism Knowhow Kits" on a variety of tourism marketing topics to help businesses improve their profits and exploit new market opportunities.

Our private sector approach is welcomed by both small and large organisations. Most of our business comes through recommendations from happy clients. We've deliberately stayed small and don't use associates or external consultants so you will know exactly who is working for you. Every project we do is different. Our shortest projects take just a day (often facilitating events or brainstorming new ideas) but we've also been retained for up to eight years.

Product Selling

The main function of a travel agency is the product sale. Product sale is very complex subject specially when the product happens to be a tourist product. Because of the special nature of the tourist product and the multiplicity of manufacturers of the product, selling assumes greater importance. In addition, the distribution channels through which the tourist product finds its way to the consumers are multiple and varied. The tourist product, consists mainly of attractions, transport and accommodation. The producers of elements of the above products include air, sea, road transport companies and carriers, hotels and other forms of accommodation units, and the organisations which are responsible for putting together attractions both natural and man-made.

In most of the countries product sale is conducted through a distribution system controlled mostly by a network of retail travel agents, tour operators and wholesalers. The individual elements of a tourist product like international air tickets, domestic air or train tickets are also mostly sold through agents or representatives of airlines and railway companies, and purchased directly by consumers. The consumers have, therefore, a choice between direct booking and using the services of an agent. In addition, there are alternative channels available to the consumers through which they may buy their tourism products. These channels include clubs and societies, mail order, travel shops in supermarkets and departmental stores, tourist fairs and exhibitions and, more recently, electronic booking methods like computers.

Circular Route

By the mid-nineteenth century 'Holidays away from home' had become customary for a larger social group than ever before. Cook's initiative and organising genius provided the final impetus. In the winter of 1850-51, Cook was already negotiating for a tour of America, but his attention was diverted when he was offered the opportunity of conducting excursion trains to the Great Exhibition of 1851. Altogether,

Cook conducted 1,65,000 people to and from the Crystal Palace. In 1856, Cook succeeded in organising his First grand circular tour of the continent. The tour was so successful that it had to be repeated six weeks later.

Thomas Cook's conquest of Europe began in 1862 when he made arrangements with Brighton and South Coast Railway for passenger traffic to the continent. Cook's Paris excursions are the first true 'package tours'; all the details of transport and accommodation were pre-arranged. In 1863 Cook visited Switzerland where his ideas were greeted with enthusiasm by hoteliers and railway proprietors. His next stop was Italy. Cook first made a personal survey of Turin, Milan, Florence and Genoa, to familiarise himself with their touristic attractions and facilities. In 1864 the first guided tour of Italy left England with applications far in excess of the available tickets. The 1860s also saw the introduction of Cook's 'railway and hotel coupons'. Cook personally examined the system by travelling through Italy to Vienna, down the Danube into Hungary and from there into Switzerland. By the 1890s, 1,200 hotels throughout the world accepted his coupons. Starting in 1868 Cook arranged regular circular tours of Switzerland and Northern Italy.

The first official London Office of Thomas Cook and Sons was established in 1865. John Mason Cook now joined his father as a permanent partner and took charge of the London office. From that year on, the history of Thomas Cook and Sons was one of continuous expansion. In the year 1880 John Mason Cook left for India and established offices in Bombay and Calcutta and formed the 'Eastern Princes' Department. In 1887 this department arranged the visits of Indian princes to Queen Victoria's Jubilee Celebrations.

By taking advantage of nineteenth century advances in transport technology, Thomas Cook and Sons had effected a revolution in tourism by the end of the century. No longer the preserve of the rich and the aristocrats, tourism was now an industry. Armed with Cook's hotel and rail coupons, the tourist could demand uniform prices and standards of service and accommodation. This new standardisation had distinct advantages. It meant comfort and convenience and less need for decision making on the part of the individual tourist. The tourist was less likely to experience discomfort or embarrassment.

The management of the Company passed on to John Mason Cook's three sons in the year 1898. At the time of John Mason Cook's death, the business included three main aspects of travel -selling tours, banking and shipping. Soon after the Second World War, the British government acquired the principal interest in the Company. In the year 1972, the British Government sold the company to Midland Bank Consortium.

Today, Thomas Cook Group is the parent company of a worldwide group of companies which are partially or wholly owned. The company also has a close trading relationship with Companie International des Wagon-Lits et Tourism, and the combined worldwide network of these companies, together with their authorised agents. The company also introduced traveller's cheques which were originally called 'circular notes'. Members of the Thomas Cook Group of companies now issue cheques as principals in different currencies and are associated with partner banks in various countries. It is also a large trader in the buying and selling of foreign currency bank notes. Thomas Cook Group Limited today provides a wide range of services to its customers in over 150 countries worldwide through their network of over 1,200 outlets. The company is considered to be one of the largest travel companies selling a wide range of travel services.

Much has changed since the year 1841, when Thomas Cook chartered a train to carry 570 travellers at a specially reduced fare from Leicester to Loughborough in England. Cook, who bought the railway tickets in bulk and resold them to members of his group, can be credited with being the first bona fide travel agent to work as a full-time professional. However, neither Thomas Cook & Sons, nor American Express Company or Cox and Kings were then a retail agent as the modern complex distribution chain had not yet evolved in any trade including travel.

Product Market

The scope and the role of the travel agency was limited in the beginning since mass tourism as we know it today had not yet begun. It was, however, the introduction of the air travel which gave a boost to the travel agency business. The introduction of an economy class by various airline companies crossing the North Atlantic heralded the era of travel agency and was responsible for their growth. The introduction of an 'economy class' in effect was nothing more than a projection of Thomas Cook's original idea of adjusting prices to encourage full capacity use of every means of transport.

Rapid development of transport system, especially the jet travel, improved living standards combined with reduction in working hours is the root cause of today's upward surge in travel. Side by side with the rapid improvements in industry and technology, practically all aspects of life have become more and more complex particularly during the past half a century. This is certainly the case in the travel industry in which, only a century ago, the job consisted almost entirely of arranging a simple reservation for the travellers in some means of transport. Today the functions and duties of a person at the travel agency counter are vastly different and more varied. He is now called upon to perform a variety of duties rather than just issue tickets and reserve seats in a train, aeroplane or accommodation in the hotel. Travel today is no longer the privilege of the few, but is sought by millions. No longer does the travel agency exist for the sole purpose of selling tickets from one point to another. The travel industry developed along certain well-defined lines as the worldwide demand on its services increased. The urge to travel became very intense over the years resulting in wide-spread growth of travel agencies in the world. Most of the travellers wished to have their travel arrangements made in advance and to be relieved of the difficulties of coping with various pre-travel arrangements of which they had only a very limited knowledge.

Recent Trends

Over the years the range and activities of a retail travel agent have increased manifold. In the modern context, the role of a travel agent is rather different to that of most of other retailers selling merchandise. The travel agent does not purchase travel with a view to reselling the same to its customers. It is only when a customer has finally decided on the purchase of travel that the agent approaches the principal on behalf of his customer. The retail travel agent, unlike most other retailers, does not carry an inventory or stock of travel products in his premises.

The main role of retail travel agents is to provide to their customers a convenient location for the "purchase" of various elements of travel like transport, accommodation and several other ancillary services associated with holiday and travel. The travel agents act as booking agents for holidays and travel and disseminate information and give advice on such services. This role can be summed up as follows:

1. To give advice to the potential tourist on the merits of alternative destinations, and
2. To make necessary arrangements for a chosen holiday which may involve booking of accommodation, transport or other relevant services associated with his travel.

A travel agent, in order to give an advice to his potential customers on the merits of a destination, must possess knowledge, expertise and up-to-date information about that destination. Besides, a travel agent has close contacts with providers of services, i.e., their principals from whom they purchase services for their customers. In other words, a retail travel agent is an intermediary providing a direct link between the consumer and the suppliers of tourist services, i.e.., airlines, transport companies, hotels, auto rental companies, etc. The retail agent is the one who acts on behalf of the principal, i.e., the original provider of tourist service such as an airline company, hotel company, shipping company, insurance company, railways or a tour operator. An agent sells the principal's services and is rewarded by a commission.

Role of Communication

In the field of travel and tourism, communication plays a very crucial role as it is through this that a potential customer obtains information about a produce which in the final analysis is a destination which he proposes to visit. Travel being a service industry the need for not only accurate but rapid information about a destination becomes paramount for the satisfaction of the consumer. The importance of communication in various fields including travel and tourism has been well recognised. World renowned space scientist, Arthur C. Clarke, addressing the first meeting of the inter-government council of the International Programme for the Development of Communication held in Paris in the year 1981, said, "In many ways and for many purposes, printed matter, books, newspapers and wallpapers will always be the best and the cheapest form of communication. But now electronics have given us tools that can perform miracles impossible to the printed word and which, of course, can reach millions who are unable to read. The newest and most powerful of these communication devices depend upon space technology, a fact that is not generally recognised."

In the period between 1981 (when Arthur Clarke spoke about the newest and most powerful communication devices) and today, with a gap of fifteen years, there has been virtually a revolution in the various techniques in the field of communication and information. The various changes that have taken place since then have greatly benefited everyone. The electronics have performed such miracles in the last two decades that today we find ourselves in the middle of a new world, a world of information revolution.

The developments have greatly facilitated rational management of the business world. Newer techniques of data processing, mainly transmission of data and telecommunication, have already formed a new field of activity, characterised by an enormous potential for growth and development. Telecommuni-cation devices are in use today in almost all fields of economy.

The new means of public telecommunication systems such as teletext, telecopy or videotex have given a very tough competition to earlier pioneer public communication means such as newspapers, magazines, etc. However, the new means of communication also offer great possibilities for improvement, rationalisation and the expansion of the existing facilities for data collection and transmission. Today the mass media world over has immensely benefited from the new technology and information techniques.

Collection of Information

The collection of information is the main part of work carried out by the journalists in connection with their work. A journalist, therefore, has to find most reliable data in as short a time as possible. Besides, the data must be the latest and up-to-date. New means of communication enable journalists to acquire the data in a short time. The data can also be obtained at any time regardless of restrictions of working hours. Hundreds of thousands of pages are stored in computers to which the journalist can have access. The data can be obtained through data banks which can be reached directly through a network that is used for most data banks.

A data bank is like a "master book" in which a mass of books, newspapers, materials from different meetings and all kinds of published work is stored. All the relevant information can be collected in no time by means of an electronic data bank. Collecting the same information from a book and a visit to a library would be time consuming and rather expensive. A journalist, seeking information on any subject for an article on tourism, can order the articles which are of interest to him, through the record room of his own editorial office, or directly through the data bank, and these are recorded on the screen. He can also acquire a written article through a directly connected printing machine. In this way, in a matter of minutes, he can finish his search and the collection of data for his article. Considerable time is saved in this way.

Chapter–8

Products of Tourism

Availability of a 'product' is the prerequisite in the marketing function. Unless there is a certain 'product', be it tangible or intangible or a service, marketing is not possible. A 'product' may be defined as the 'Sum of the physical and psychological satisfactions it provides to the buyer'. 'Marketing' by definition is the development of a product to meet the needs of the consumer and then employing the techniques of direct sales, publicity and advertising to bring this product to the consumer.

For a tourist product, the basic raw materials are the country's natural beauty, climate, history, culture and the people. Other aspects are the existing facilities necessary for comfortable living such as water supply, electricity, roads, transport, communication and other essentials. In other words the tourist product can be seen as a composite product, as the sum-total of a country's tourist attractions, transport, accommodation and the entertainment which hopefully result in consumer satisfaction. The tourist product can be entirely a man-made one or nature's creation improved upon by man. Each of these components of a tourist product is supplied by individual providers of services like hotel companies, airlines or other suppliers, and is offered directly to the tourist by them. A consumer can combine these individual tourist products through a large number of ways.

There would be many possible destinations, each with a number of hotels, each to be reached by more than one airline. Thus the potential choice before the consumer is very large.

Competing destinations have placed at the disposal of a tourist a large variety of tourist products in abundant quantity. This eventually has led to the adoption of the new concept, i.e., the marketing concept in tourism by various countries promoting tourism. The important point about marketing is that it applies to situations where the choice can be limited to a relatively small number of brands giving the consumer a reasonable choice. The process of selection thus becomes easier. In the field of tourism this process is taking place by the increasing use of 'package tours'. A package tour is a travel plan which includes most elements of vacation, such as transportation, accommodation, sightseeing and entertainment. The tourist product is a composite product, whether it is sold as a package or assembled by the individual tourist himself or his travel agent. The tourist product can, therefore, be analysed in terms of:

1. Attractions
2. Facilities
3. Accessibility.

Of the three basic components of a tourist product, "attractions" are very important. Unless these are there, the tourists will not be motivated to go to a particular place. Attractions are those elements in the tourist product which determine the choice of a particular tourist to visit one particular destination rather than another. The attractions could be cultural like sites and areas of archaeological interest, historical buildings and monuments or scenic like flora and fauna, beach resorts, mountains, national parks or events like trade fairs, exhibitions, arts and music festivals, games, etc. Facilities are those elements in the tourist product which are a necessary aid to the tourist centre. The facilities complement the attractions. These include accommodations, various types of entertainments, picnic sites, recreation and so on. These are indeed important for every tourist centre. "Accessibility" is a means by which a tourist can reach the area where attractions are located. Tourist attractions of whatever type would be of little importance if their locations are inaccessible by the normal means of transport. If the tourist attractions are located at places where no means of transport can reach, or where there are inadequate transport facilities, these become of little value. The tourist attractions which are located near to the tourist generating markets and are linked by a network of efficient transport, receive the maximum number of tourists.

Special Features

Although general principles of marketing of products of other industries could be applicable to marketing of tourist product, there are certain differences in the approach. These differences are because of the peculiar character of the tourist product. The following are the peculiarities of a tourist product.

Intangible Non-Material : No transfer of ownership of goods is involved as compared to a tangible product, e.g., a motor car. In tourism, instead, certain facilities, installations, items of equipment are made available for a specified time and for a specified use. For instance, a seat in an aeroplane or a train for a journey from one point to another or a booking in a hotel through a travel agent is carried out for a customer, or services such as information and advice are provided.

Production and Consumption

The travel agent or tour operator who sells his product cannot store it. Production can only take place or can only be completed if the customer is actually present. There is a close link between production and consumption of tourist services. Most tourist services cannot be consumed incrementally. In other words, consumption, once begun, cannot be stopped, interrupted or modified at all. As a result, risk and uncertainty for the customer are higher, and his need for reliable pre-purchase information is stronger. The potential customer's decision-risk and dependence on accurate information are further increased because he cannot see, inspect, compare or try out tourist services before deciding to use them.

Assembled by Many Producers : The tourist product cannot be provided by a single enterprise. Each of the components of a tourist product is highly specialised and together make the final product. This is not so in the case of other tangible products where one manufacturer produces a total product. In tourism, on the other hand, an airline considers 'seats flown' or passenger miles to be its product, a hotel produces 'guest nights', a travel agent 'bookings', a theatre and museum or an archaeological site measures its 'production' in numbers of visitors. In the tourist's view, however, the product he buys covers the complete experience of his visit to a particular place. In other words, the tourist product is not an airline or a rail seat, or a hotel bed or a theatre ticket, but rather an amalgam of many components which together make a complete product. Because of these peculiar characteristics, coordination in marketing efforts is very crucial.

Tourism Product Development Idea

The tourism industry like any other industry is striving to attain a competitive advantage in an increasingly complex world. Achieving such an advantage is increasingly tied to knowledge, know-how, and other intangibles. Organisations that intend to stay ahead in their field must take the necessary steps to identify their assets and use them to their best advantage. Tourism departments and travel agencies have to generate new ideas for diversification of tourism products, packages and circuits along with qualitative and quantitative changes in their packages. It is profitable to prepare packages based on their core competence i.e., the strengths of individual states rather than a generalized mix.

India is, and has always been a storehouse of intellectual and cultural wisdom and her diversity, cultural richness, and multifarious ways of living place her in a unique position of being able to offer many culturally distinctive products to the global community.

The rich cultural heritage of India, which has always evoked a sense of great awe among people all over the world, is vast and varied in scope. India's achievements are highly original as revealed through its art and architecture, religion and philosophy, language and literature, music

India can use the rich potential offered by its people and their customs, ancient myths and legends, colorful rites and rituals, festivals, and pilgrim centers for achieving diversification of tourism products, packages and circuits. Proper research conducted in these areas will provide new insights to those who are actively involved in tourism introduction of qualitative and quantitative changes in their packages. This will create 'Special Tourism Areas' for investment and development, which will reduce the burden on existing circuits.industry and other industries related to tourism.

The cultural attractions can be classified as hard and soft. The former includes historical sites, museums, architecture, monuments, religious buildings and archaeological sites while the latter consists of music, drama, poetry, literature, painting, sculpture engravings, herbal medicines, folklore, handicrafts or even heritage walks. Both have to be imaginatively combined. Tourism packages should combine one cultural medium with another and incorporate a whole range of lectures, presentations, demonstrations etc.

Tourism products based on cultural heritage are unending. Packages may range from Emperor 'Ashoka', 'Ayurveda', 'Museums', 'Game of Chess', 'Poetry' to specific 'Sculptures'-the list is endless. The products based on cultural heritage accentuate the relevance of national heritage to everyday life. Cultural attractions should be interpreted in such a way as to make them living, vibrant and entertaining. This process of interpretation in tourism is essential. It adds to the quality of the experience by adding to the way in which tourists are informed and the degree to which their interest is stimulated.

The skills and knowledge of a tourist guide alone are not enough. Interpretation must adopt a multi-media approach to the reconstruction of the past by including video presentations, talks and lectures, regular guided tours, music and poetry recitals, guided trails and walks, books and published information, posters and postcards, and other printed material, special displays and exhibitions, signboards and explanatory notices. It is a holistic approach.

Tourism markets tend to talk about the new traveler who may be described as cultural traveler. The new traveler is described as better educated, more culturally aware and sensitive, and more curious and analytical. Such travelers look for an alternative to the large mass tourism markets. They do not want large, modern hotels constructed and equipped according to international norms. They want to stay in small locally owned accommodation units, very much a part of the local community and reflecting local values and ways of life. This provides an opportunity to the tourism industry to feature and protect local culture and to involve the community in such a way that local people benefit fully.

Cultural tourism products are to be developed so that they assimilate and support local needs and aspirations. These new products must promote local cuisine, the use of local materials and handicrafts, and develop a whole range of other participating tourism services viz. local folkloric performances, handicrafts demonstrations, and cultural and recreational activities, heritage walks etc. It must also encourage the creation and development of tourism enterprises operated and owned by local people.

Tourism product at the destination comprises all those attractions, facilities, and services used or visited during a stay. It also comprises everything that happens to visitors, everything they experience. Tourism product consists of both tangible and intangible components. The natural, cultural and historical resources, infrastructure and superstructure are tangible. They can be evaluated, measured and subjected to specific standards of provision while the intangible aspects cannot be. They come together to form the atmosphere of a place and its aura of hospitality and friendliness. The intangible elements can be said to give the tourist product its life, colour and excitement. All of the tangible aspects, however good, cannot guarantee satisfaction. The way tourists are treated and how they feel, influences decisively their overall reaction to a place.

The image builds up over the years and it is a product of history, of cultural influences, and also of myth and legend. Who else goes there and what they say about it also influences the image of a destination. Leading personalities may speak well of a place. If a well-known transnational companies sets up operations in a country, it contributes to enhancing the reputation of the place. If major tour operators feature it as a part of their programs, this too contributes to a positive image. It is built up over time, as the result of a constant flow of messages and stimuli. It should be kept at the forefront; people have to keep writing and talking about a product. Once people visit a place they will form their own impressions. They will take an image away with them. What they say and the personal recommendations they make affects the product.

Chapter–9

Tourist Destination

A tourist destination is a city, town, or other area that is dependent to a significant extent on the revenues accruing from tourism. It may contain one or more tourist attractions and possibly some "tourist traps." These tourist destinations are represented in the United States by Convention and Visitor Bureaus (CVB's), which are paid by bed taxes to market the destinations to travelers.

Choice of the Destination

Incentive trips are of two types. These are the 'Dealer Trips' and 'Sales Force Trips'. Dealer Trips as a general rule are of slightly longer duration as compared to 'Sales Force Trips' and are more likely to use offshore sites. These are likely to be oriented to pleasure and relaxation and to have little or no business content. On the other hand 'Sales Force Trips' tend to be of shorter duration favouring domestic sites and having some business content.

Assuming that the choice comes down to several equally attractive sites, the following factors influence the choice of the buyers:

1. *Budget:* Although a crucial factor yet not necessarily a limiting factor.

2. *Period of the Year:* Each industry has a 'slow season' when its people can get away easily on incentive trips.
3. *Incentive History* : Few holiday sites are repeatable in a five-year period, and even then, there must be a gap between the first and the second trip.
4. Demographics of the winners, varying sophistication of incentive winners must be considered.
5. *Accessibility:* Incentive travel users need assurance that they can bring their groups into a destination in comfort and without any hassles.
6. *Facilities* : All necessary facilities like hotel rooms, conference rooms, restaurants, entertainment should be available at the destination.

Tourism in Australia: Case Study

Tourism in Australia is a large sector of the economy. In 2003/04, the tourism industry represented 3.9% of Australia's GDP at a value of approximately A$32 billion to the national economy. Tourism's share of GDP has been slightly decreasing over recent years. 1.1% of total exports of goods and services.

At least until September 2001, tourism and particularly international tourism had grown rapidly for the past two decades. 5.7 million tourists visited Australia for the year ending April 2010.

During 2001–2002 and 2002–2003, external events such as the September 11 attacks and the Severe Acute Respiratory Syndrome (SARS) scare caused changes to the level of international visitors to Australia. The internal event of the collapse of the country's second biggest airline Ansett Australia also led to a decline in tourism.

All visitors to Australia, apart from New Zealanders, require advance permission to enter the country. For most countries, a full visa is required, but holders of certain passports from some OECD and some East Asian countries are able to apply for the simpler Electronic Travel Authority which enables one to apply and be granted a visa.

Australia's international tourism campaigns have focused on Australia's laid-back style, such as an 1980s advertising campaign featuring actor Paul Hogan telling American tourists "I'll slip an extra shrimp on the barbie for you", or its cheeky side, as in its controversial 2006 campaign in the United Kingdom using the Australian colloquialism slogan "So where the bloody hell are you?".

The latest campaign "New York" and "Shanghai" was launched on the 8th of October 2008. The two television commercials are being rolled out in 22 countries. Eleven print advertisements, shot in every Australian State and Territory, have been produced in conjunction with DDB Worldwide, Tourism Australia's new advertising agency. DDB will produce Tourism Australia's next international campaign to be rolled out post-June 2009.

Japanese tourists make up a distinctive part of the Australian tourism market, usually taking short package tours which concentrate heavily on the iconic sights (typically Sydney, Uluru, Gold Coast and Cairns), and viewing Australian native animals (particularly the koala). Another major source of tourists to Australia include backpackers, mostly young people from Western European countries (particularly the United Kingdom) and North America. Spending more time in Australia, these travellers tend to explore considerably more of the country. Many backpackers participate in working holidays enabling them to stay longer in the country. Working holiday visas for Australia are available for those aged 18 to 30 for most Western European citizens, and also citizens of Canada and some developed East Asian nations such as Japan and South Korea.

Australians are big domestic travellers as well, with a profusion of seaside resort towns in every state (many located on or near good surfing beaches), mountain retreats, plentiful national parks, rivers, fishing locations, wine growing regions, as well as domestic visitation of the major tourist spots. Domestic tourism peaks during the Australian school holidays.

The 2003 Rugby World Cup attracted 65000 international visitors to Australia. The 2000 Sydney Olympics resulted in significant inbound and domestic tourism to Sydney. During the games, Sydney hosted 362,000 domestic and 110,000 international visitors. In addition, up to 4 billion people watched the games worldwide.

Tourism in Sydney

Tourism in Sydney, Australia forms an important part of the city's economy. The city received 22.6 million domestic visitors and 2.7 million international visitors in year ending Dec 2009. The most well known attractions include the Sydney Opera House, and the Sydney Harbour Bridge. Other attractions include Royal Botanical Gardens, Luna Park, the beaches and Sydney Tower.

Tourism Promotion—The New South Wales Government operates two relevant programs relevant to Sydney as part of the NSW Tourism Strategy:

1. *Brand Sydney* - Revitalise and strengthen the image and appeal of Sydney.
2. *Visit Sydney* - To increase promotion of Sydney as a tourist destination through a strengthened dedicated business unit within Tourism NSW.

Brand Sydney—Brand Sydney project will be led by the Premier of New South Wales, overseen by the Minister for Tourism and a Project Steering Committee and delivered by the Project Team. Sports administrator John O'Neill is the chair of Brand Sydney.

Sydney Harbour—Port Jackson is the natural harbour of Sydney. It is known for its spectacular natural beauty, and in particular as the location of the Sydney Opera House and Sydney Harbour Bridge. The area around the harbour foreshore contains pockets of bushland which was once common around Sydney, containing a surprising range of native animals.

Sydney Opera House—The Sydney Opera House is one of the most distinctive and famous 20th century buildings, and one of the most famous performing arts venues in the world. Situated on Bennelong Point in Sydney Harbour, with parkland to its south and close to the equally famous Sydney Harbour Bridge, the building and its surroundings form an iconic Australian image. It was included in the Olympic Torch route in 2000 to the Olympic stadium. It was the backdrop of some events for the Sydney 2000 Olympics, including the triathlon—which began at the Opera House—and the yachting events on Sydney Harbour. The dramatic exteriors have not been matched with technically superior interiors, and the Opera House's reputation as a music venue has suffered as a result.

Sydney Harbour Bridge—The Sydney Harbour Bridge is the main crossing of Sydney Harbour carrying rail, vehicular, and pedestrian traffic between the Sydney central business district (CBD) and the North Shore. The dramatic water vista of the bridge together with the nearby Sydney Opera House is an iconic image of both Sydney and Australia. The South-east pylon for many years operated as lookout and tourist attraction, containing a number of telescopes and antiquated arcade games which operated on pennies, long after that currency had gone out of operation. The pylon has recently been renovated and returned to its tourist function.

Bridge Climb—Since 1998, BridgeClimb has made it possible for tourists to climb the southern half of the bridge. Tours run throughout the day, from dawn to dusk and are only cancelled for electrical storms or high wind. Night climbs are also available. Groups of climbers are provided with protective clothing appropriate to the prevailing weather conditions and are given an orientation before climbing. During the climb, attendees are secured to the bridge by a wire lifeline. Each climb begins on the eastern side of the bridge and ascends to the top. At the summit, the group crosses to the western side of the arch for the descent. Each climb is a three-and-a-half-hour experience.

Historic Forts—The shores of Sydney Harbour are home to a number of historic batteries, bunkers and forts, many of which are now heritage listed. Some of these forts date back to 1871 and were part of Sydney Harbours defence system that was designed to withstand a seaborn attack. There are four historical fortifications located between Bradleys Head and Middle Head on the north side of the harbour; the Middle Head Fortifications, the Georges Head Battery, the Lower Georges Heights Commanding Position and a small fort located on Bradleys Head. The forts were constructed from mostly large sandstone blocks and consist of many tunnels, catacombs and underground rooms.

Watsons Bay—Watsons Bay sits on the end of the South Head peninsula and takes its name from the sheltered bay and anchorage on its western side, in Port Jackson. It provides some of the best views across the harbour to the city of Sydney and the Harbour Bridge. The Gap is an ocean cliff on the eastern side with views to Manly, North Head, and the Pacific Ocean.

Watsons Bay is a mostly residential area with some recreational areas and beaches, including one legal nude beach. Some restaurants, cafes and the Watsons Bay Hotel are located here, with Doyles on the Beach, one of the Sydney's most famous seafood restaurants, located on the foreshore of Watsons Bay. The naval base HMAS *Watson* is located nearby at South Head.

City of Sydney

The Rocks—The Rocks is an inner-city suburb, tourist precinct and historic area of Sydney. It is located on the southern shore of Sydney Harbour adjacent to the city centre, close to where Sydney was first settled in 1788. The close proximity to Circular Quay and the views of the iconic Harbour Bridge, as well as the historic nature of many of the buildings, mean that the Rocks is very popular with tourists. It features a variety of souvenir and craft shops, and many themed and historic pubs. The Rocks Market operates each weekend, with around 100 stalls. There are numerous historic walks through the area, visiting historical buildings such as Cadman's Cottage, Sydney Observatory, and the Dawes Point Battery, which was the first fortified position in New South Wales.

Sydney Tower—Sydney Tower is Sydney's tallest free-standing structure, and the second tallest in Australia, the Q1 building on the Gold Coast being the tallest. It is also the second tallest observation tower in the Southern Hemisphere after Auckland, New Zealand's Sky Tower; though Sydney Tower's main observation deck is almost 50 metres higher than that of the Sky Tower. The Sydney Tower is a member of the World Federation of Great Towers. It is known by locals as the Centrepoint Tower, after the shopping centre building the tower sprouts from.

Sydney Tower Skywalk, or just Skywalk, is an open-air, glass-floored platform circling Sydney Tower at a height of 260m above ground level. The moving viewing platform extends out over the edge of the main structure of Sydney Tower. This attraction is more than twice as high as the popular BridgeClimb walk to the top of Sydney Harbour Bridge. From the platform the seaward horizon is 58 kilometres away, although inland features such as the Blue Mountains can be seen at further distances. See Sydney Attractions Group.

Darling Harbour—Darling Harbour was redeveloped from an industrial wharf to a major tourist and retail precinct in 1988, and is home to a number of major public facilities and attractions, including:

1. Sydney Entertainment Centre
2. Sydney's Chinese Gardens
3. Tumbalong Park
4. Sydney Convention and Exhibition Centre
5. Australian National Maritime Museum (featuring museum ships including HMAS Vampire)
6. Star City Casino
7. Sydney Aquarium
8. the IMAX theatre
9. Wildlife World.

The Darling Harbour precinct is linked to the CBD by the Sydney Monorail and Pyrmont Bridge.

Kings Cross—The Kings Cross area is infamous in Australia as being a red light district, similar to Kings Cross, London with numerous strip clubs and "girlie" bars along Darlinghurst Road, although the demographics have changed in recent years and gentrification of the area has led to clashes between new and established elements. Kings Cross is also known for its Neon signs and advertising posters, the most famous being the iconic Coca-Cola sign. It is often affectionately referred to by Sydneysiders by the colloquialism "the Cross".

The Kings Cross district was the City of Sydney's bohemian heartland from the early decades of the 20th Century, but due its proximity to the naval docking area at Garden Island it also came to serve as the city's main tourist accommodation and entertainment centre, as well as its red-light district. The drugs and crime associated with this trade led to Kings Cross achieving a high level of notoriety.

Museums—Sydney is home to a number of established museums. The Australian Museum is the oldest museum in Australia, and is particularly renowned in the fields of natural history and anthropology. The Museum of Sydney is located in Australia's first Government House, and its permanent and temporary exhibitions highlight the history of the city. The Powerhouse Museum specialises in science and technology, and its exhibits include the oldest steam engine in the world with a rotating action that is still in operation. The Australian National Maritime Museum focuses on Australia's maritime history.

City Parks—Hyde Park contains well-kept gardens and approximately 580 trees; a mixture of Moreton Bay Figs, Palms and other varieties. It is famed for its magnificent fig tree lined avenues, a peaceful haven in the business heart of the city. At the park's southern end is the ANZAC War Memorial and a monument consisting of a 104-millimetre gun from the German light cruiser SMS *Emden*. The Royal Botanic Gardens is the largest of three major botanical gardens open to the public in Sydney. Admission is free and it is open to the public every day of the year.

Beaches—Sydney is renowned for its beaches and, with its warm climate, attracts people to the beaches almost all year round.

Bondi Beach—Sydney's most famous beach attracts large numbers of tourists to Bondi throughout the year with many Irish and British tourists spending Christmas Day there. Bondi Beach features many popular cafes, restaurants and hotels, some with spectacular views of the beach and surrounding headlands. The beach itself is approximately one kilometre long.

Manly Beach—Manly Beach is a well known beach situated at the southern end of Sydney's Northern Beaches. Manly Beach's access to the city via a 30 minute ride on Sydney's ferries makes it popular with tourists and is host to a number of international surfing events.

Wildlife

Taronga Zoo—Taronga is the city zoo of Sydney, officially opened on October 7, 1916. It is located on the shores of Sydney Harbour in Mosman. Taronga is linked to Dubbo's Western Plains Zoo in terms of breeding programs. Taronga Zoo is home to over 2,600 animals on 28.7 hectares, making it one of the largest of its kind, and it divided into eight zoogeographic regions with numerous indoor pavilions and outdoor exhibits. Taronga Zoo has about 340 species and over 2600 individual animals. They are housed in a large variety of exhibits.

Sydney Wildlife World—Sydney Wildlife World is a zoo in the Sydney CBD. It officially opened in September 2006. It is located on the shores of Darling Harbour and is attached to Sydney Aquarium. Sydney Wildlife World is unusual for a zoo in that it is entirely enclosed and air-conditioned. The indoor zoo features a one-kilometre walkway which snakes through 7000 square metres of enclosures. The enclosure features around 6000 native animals.

Whale Watching—Sydney's coastline is part of the annual group 5 Humpback migration path from Antarctica to the Coral sea. From mid May to Early December they can be seen in the waters of the coast and on rare occasions swimming into Sydney Harbour itself. Whale Watching can be done from any of the clifftop walks or lookouts, however there are volunteer locations at North Head and Cape Solander at Botany Bay and a number of boat based whale watching tours departing from the Sydney CBD.

Sydney Suburbs and Daytrips

Centennial Park area—Centennial Park is located 4km south east of the city. It is traditional European parkland, laid out for the centenary of European settlement in 1888. It is suited for family picnics, horse riding, sightseeing, scenic walks. Adjacent to Centennial Park is the Entertainment Quarter which has cinemas and restaurants.

Sydney Olympic Park—Sydney Olympic Park is a 640-hectare site located adjacent to the suburb of Homebush Bay, New South Wales, Australia. It was built for the 2000 Olympics and continues to be used for sporting and cultural events, including the Sydney Royal Easter Show, Sydney Festival, Big Day Out and a number of world class sporting fixtures. It is served by the Olympic Park railway station. There are also regular services to the nearby wharf which operate from various points around Sydney Harbour.

Blue Mountains—The Blue Mountains National Park is one of the most popular parks in Australia. The majority of tourists to the Blue Mountains see the National Park from one of the many lookouts between Wentworth Falls and Blackheath, and many of these never actually set foot in the park.

Despite this, there are many activities for the visitor. Short walks to impressive lookouts above cliff and waterfalls abound. Overnight and longer walks allow access to some of the more remote areas of the park. Other popular activities include canyoning and mountain biking.

Tourism in Melbourne

Melbourne, Australia, is an important tourist destination with approximately 15.9 million domestic and 1.4 million international tourists visiting Melbourne in year ending Dec 2009. Melbourne attracts a wide cross-section of visitors, who come for a variety of reasons. Major sporting events hosted by Melbourne have attracted large numbers of sports tourists to the city, other visitors come for the cultural and fashion events. In 2008, Melbourne exceeded Sydney for the first time in terms of money spent by domestic tourists on a per capita basis while in total amounts Melbourne earned considerable less.

Popular Sites and Events—Melbourne has a large number of events and attractions which are available throughout the year, These include:

1. Federation Square is a major meeting place in Melbourne. It is close to Flinders Street Station, the MCG and various other sporting and cultural venues. The square includes several buildings, housing the NGV Australia and the Australian Centre for the Moving Image, as well as exhibition spaces, auditoria, restaurants, bars and shops. Large crowds frequently watch concerts, cultural and various sporting events on the square's large electronic screen located in one of two public areas. Adjacent to the Square is Birrarung Marr, a park on the banks of the Yarra. The main Tourist Information Centre is located in the Square. You can obtain a large range of tourist brochures here including guided walking tours of Melbourne.
2. The Melbourne Cricket Ground, known as "the MCG" or simply the "G" has the largest capacity of any Australian sporting stadium. The MCG was the centerpiece stadium of the 1956 Summer Olympic Games and was renovated in preparation for the 2006 Commonwealth Games, increasing the stadium's capacity to 103,000. From April to September, the stadium typically hosts one or two Australian rules football matches each week. It has also hosted two Bledisloe Cup rugby matches. During the summer, major cricket matches including the Boxing Day test match and several one-day international games are played there.
3. Eureka Skydeck, is the highest viewing platform in the southern hemisphere and is located in Eureka Tower. Eureka Tower is the tallest residential building in the world. The observation deck includes

a glass cube ride that projects three meters from the side of the building.

4. The Melbourne Observation Deck, located some 237 metres above the city streets on the 55th floor of the Rialto Towers, offers spectacular views of the central business district and beyond. The Rialto Towers is the second tallest building in Melbourne after Eureka Tower.
5. Melbourne Park is the home of the Australian Open tennis tournament. Held every January, it is one of the four Grand Slam tournaments.
6. The Melbourne Exhibition and Convention Centre is located in Southbank and was built in the 1990s as a replacement for the Royal Exhibition Building. It has hosted conventions and exhibitions since its opening.
7. The Melbourne Museum is located on the north-eastern fringe of the CBD, next to the Royal Exhibition Building. To many Melburnians, the most significant exhibit is the preserved body of Phar Lap, a famous racehorse of the Depression era. The Forest Gallery is a living internal facsimile replicating the forests of the nearby Dandenong Ranges. CSIRAC, the fifth electronic computer built and the only one of its generation to survive intact is also on display. The museum complex is also home to Melbourne's IMAX cinema.
8. The Royal Exhibition Building located in the Carlton Gardens was built in the 1880s for the World's Fair and is only one of a few such buildings that still exist. The building and gardens were granted World Heritage listing on 2 July 2004. It is the first building in Australia to be granted this status. The building also held the first sitting of the Australian Parliament on 9 May 1901. Subsequent federal parliamentary

sittings were then moved to the Victorian Parliament building located in Spring Street and the Victorian government moved to the Exhibition Building.

9. The State Library of Victoria on Swanston Street, with its large Domed Reading Room and statue-filled front lawn.
10. The National Gallery of Victoria possesses the largest art collection in Australia. The gallery operates from two sites: one housing the Australian collection at the Ian Potter Centre: NGV Australia at Federation Square (notably featuring key works from the Heidelberg School); and the NGV International collection housed in the main St Kilda Road building.
11. The Victorian Arts Centre at Southgate is a Melbourne landmark with its enormous skyward spire. It hosts Opera Australia's Melbourne season, the Melbourne Symphony Orchestra, the Melbourne Theatre Company, the Australian Ballet Company, Chunky Move (one of Australia's best-known contemporary dance companies), and other touring productions. The centre consists of two separate buildings: the State Theatre; and Hamer Hall (this was recently re-named in honour of the late former premier Sir Rupert Hamer. The acoustics of the Centre are often favourably compared with those of its interstate rival, the opera theatre in the Sydney Opera House.
12. Crown Casino on the Yarra River is the largest gambling centre in the southern hemisphere. The Crown Entertainment Complex also encompasses one of Melbourne's best hotels the Crown Towers, restaurants, boutiques and cinemas. Crown also has the Palladium Ballroom which hosts some of Melbourne's biggest events, such as the Logies and the Brownlow Medal AFL award.

13. The Melbourne Aquarium contains a variety of exhibits showcasing marine wildlife found in the Southern Ocean and the Antarctic.
14. The Shrine of Remembrance on St Kilda Road is one of Australia's largest war memorials. It is the site of annual observances of ANZAC Day and Remembrance Day.
15. Docklands is Melbourne's newest precinct and largest infrastructure development to date, and is also becoming a major tourist attraction. The Docklands area opens up the waterfront to the CBD and is projected to attract millions of visitors every year. Telstra Dome, the Southern Star Observation Wheel, public art displays and several dining precincts can be found in Docklands.
16. Glow Golf at Dockland is an indoor Glow in the Dark Black light indoor Mini Golf based on an Australiana theme, 18 holes of fun and challenge whatever the weather. open September 2009.
17. Luna Park Melbourne is an amusement park located on the foreshore of Port Phillip Bay in St Kilda, an inner suburb of Melbourne. It has been operating since 1912.

Restaurants—Melbourne is also noted for the number, variety and quality of its restaurants. Major restaurant strips are found throughout the city and the suburbs, including:

1. Chinatown, on Little Bourke Street and now spreading out onto Russell Street in the CBD, offers numerous restaurants, mainly but not exclusively offering Cantonese cuisine, at the lower end offering Hong Kong-style noodle restaurants up to the Flower Drum, renowned for its Peking Duck and is generally regarded as Melbourne's best restaurant.
2. Lygon Street, in the inner-northern suburb of Carlton, offers a selection of mainly Italian-influenced food.

3. Brunswick Street in inner-suburban Fitzroy used to be a grungy hotbed of students, musicians, actors and the like, and still retains some remnant of that edginess with the presence of several live music venues, all manner of eclectic stores, accompanied by restaurants and cafes, many of which serve varied and contemporary menus.
4. Chapel Street, south of the city is a popular destination for fashionable clothes shopping, eating and entertainment. The long street contains commercial areas providing goods and services for local residents. Chapel Street intersects with Toorak Road, itself offering entertainment, food and shops.
5. Glenferrie Road, east of the city in inner suburban Malvern has a wide mix of different cuisines including Indian, Malaysian, Thai and Japanese. The street intersects with High Street in Armadale which also has a mix of antique shops, cafes and restaurants.
6. Glenhuntly Road, south east of the city in inner suburban Elsternwick is a busy strip that offers a wide range of different restaurant cuisines including Chinese, Malaysian Indian, Thai, and some Middle Eastern cuisines.
7. Nelson Place faces the water in Williamstown, and is especially popular for lazy weekend breakfasts and lunches. There are restaurants and cafes featuring the usual range of cuisines, and footpath tables outside many of the establishments.

Cafes and Nightlife—Melbourne contains all manner of pubs, bars, and nightclubs. The CBD contains a wide variety of venues, from the ubiquitous faux-Irish pubs and more traditional Aussie hotels, through some very upmarket wine bars, serious jazz venues on Bennetts Lane, fashionable nightclubs and dance venues (where the Melbourne Shuffle was born), are often hidden away down obscure grungy alleys.

The restaurant strips, particularly Brunswick Street have their own bars, some of which are the best rock venues in Melbourne. King Street, on the southern side of the CBD, was traditionally a nightclub strip and still hosts several, but many are now exotic dancing venues. Chapel Street, Prahran, is perhaps the trendiest, most upmarket nightlife strip. Bayside St Kilda is the home of several huge music venues including the famous Esplanade Hotel (known as 'the Espy'), the Prince of Wales, and The Palace.

The recent influx of city-dwellers has given rise to the numerous underground bars and sidewalk cafes in the alleys between Flinders Street - Flinders Lane and Bourke Street - Lonsdale Street. Notable alleys include Block Arcade/Block Place, Degraves Street, and Hardware Lane.

Other prominent cafe strips include:

1. St Kilda's Fitzroy Street, Carlisle Street and Acland Street are home to many popular cafes.
2. Fitzroy's Brunswick Street
3. South Yarra's Chapel Street
4. Collingwood's Smith Street
5. Richmond's Bridge Road
6. Southbank's Southgate and Crown Casino.

Melbourne also has a vibrant gay community, with gay and gay-friendly bars across the city. It is mostly concentrated on two gay villages - Commercial Rd, South Yarra and Smith St, Collingwood, but there are also gay bars and clubs in St Kilda, Fitzroy, Richmond and Yarraville.

Close to Melbourne—There are a variety of interesting things to see outside Melbourne proper but still within a day trip of Melbourne:

1. The Yarra valley region, producer of high-quality wine and with beautiful rainforest scenery nearby.

2. The Mornington Peninsula, with its wineries, beaches and the Arthurs Seat lookout.
3. The Surf Coast near Geelong, with excellent surf beaches and the spectacular views of the Great Ocean Road (Voted the world's best road trip in 2003).
4. Ballarat, a small city once the centre of the gold rush and site of the Eureka Stockade.
5. Bendigo.
6. Phillip Island, home of the Australian Motorcycle Grand Prix, also has one of the few easily-accessible colonies of little penguins.
7. French Island in Western Port Bay
8. Geelong, 80 kilometres (50 mi) down the Princes Hwy is the gateway to many of Australia's tourist destinations such as the Great Ocean Road, Twelve Apostles and Bells Beach. Geelong is famous for its world class waterfront on on Corio Bay. One of the largest waterfront redevelopments ever undertaken in Australia, Waterfront Geelong includes Cunningham Pier with its Smorgy's restaurant, a Carousel Pavilion, and the art-deco bathing area at Eastern Beach.
9. Gippsland region, home of the Gourmet Deli Tours, the Gippsland Lakes, Wilsons Promontory (with South Point, the most southerly point of the Australian mainland), and many picturesque towns such as Sale, Foster, Bairnsdale, Lakes Entrance, and Warragul - one of the richest dairy farming areas in Australia. The ghost town of Walhalla is filled with goldmining memorabilia.
10. Dandenong Ranges are famous for the Puffing Billy steam train in Belgrave, a large suburb of Melbourne, the Dandenong Ranges are located less than 30 kilometres (19 mi) from Melbourne with beautiful

townships of Mount Dandenong, Olinda, Upwey, Sassafrass and the commercial, residential and large "capitals", Belgrave and Ferntree Gully, the Dandenongs are also known for the view of the sun setting over Melbourne.

CHAPTER–10

THE ATTRACTIONS

A tourist attraction is a place of interest where tourists visit, typically for its inherent or exhibited cultural value, historical significance, natural or built beauty, or amusement opportunities. Some examples include historical places, monuments, zoos, aquaria, museums and art galleries, botanical gardens, buildings and structures (e.g., castles, libraries, former prisons, skyscrapers, bridges), national parks and forests, theme parks and carnivals, living history museums, ethnic enclave communities, historic trains and cultural events. Many tourist attractions are also landmarks.

Tourist attractions are also created to capitalise on legends such as a supposed UFO crash site near Roswell, New Mexico and the alleged Loch Ness monster sightings in Scotland. Ghost sightings also make tourist attractions. Ethnic communities may become tourist attractions, such as Chinatowns in the United States and the black British neighborhood of Brixton in London, England.

In the US, owners and marketers of attractions advertise tourist attractions on billboards along the side of highways and roadways, especially in remote areas. Tourist attractions often provide free promotional brochures and flyers in information centres, fast food restaurants, hotel and motel rooms or lobbies, and rest areas. While some tourist attractions provide visitors a memorable experience for a reasonable admission charge or even for free, others can have a tendency to be of low quality and to overprice their goods and services (such as admission, food, and souvenirs) in order to profit from tourists excessively. Such places are commonly known as tourist traps.

Land Tourist Attractions

Amusement Parks	Castles	Horseback Riding	Racquetball Courts
Apple Picking	Caves	Horseshoes	Rain Forests
Aquariums	Cemeteries	Hunting	Recreation Centers
Arcades	Croquet	Ice Skating	Roller Skating
Art Galleries	Cross Country Skiing	Laser Tag	Safaris
Auctions	Cycling	Libraries	Shuffle Board
Basketball Courts	Dog Parks	Mansions	Skateboard Parks
Billiards Pool Halls	Dog Sledding	Memorials	Skiing
Bingo	Expeditions	Miniature Golf	Snowboarding
Bird Watching	Fairs	Monuments	Snowmobiling
Bocce Ball Courts	Fitness Centers	Mountain Biking	Spas
Bowling	Flea Markets	Mountain Climbing	Tennis Courts
Bridges	Frisbee Golf Frolf	Museums	Tours
Bungee Jumping	Gardens	National and State Parks	Train Rides
Butterfly Watching	Go Carts	Paintball	Volcanoes
Camping	Gold Panning	Parks	Waterfalls
Car Shows	Golf Courses	Picnic Areas	Wine Tasting
Carnivals	Gun Ranges	Planetariums	Zoos
Casinos	Hiking	Poker Rooms	

North America Tourist Attractions
United States Tourist Attractions
Arizona AZ Tourist Attractions
Sedona Tourist Attractions

Tourist Attraction Category	Tourist Attraction Type	Venue Name	Attraction Review	Hours of Operation	Price Range	Ratings	Value Ratings	Tourist Attraction Description
Land Tourist Attractions	Spas	Stillpoint...Living in Balance	Stillpoint...Living in Balance Review	Morning to Evening	$100	Not Rated	Not Rated	Sedona's premier massage therapy, energetic balancing, and body/mind practice. Voted Best Sedona Massage Therapists.

California CA Tourist Attractions
Santa Rosa Tourist Attractions

Tourist Attraction Category	Tourist Attraction Type	Venue Name	Attraction Review	Hours of Operation	Price Range	Rating	Value Rating	Tourist Attraction Description
Land Tourist Attractions	Tours	Up & Away Ballooning	Up & Away Ballooning Review	Morning Only	$200	Not Rated	Not Rated	Hot air balloon rides in Sonoma County. Only company in the U.S. offering wheelchair accessible basket.

Maine ME Tourist Attractions
Fort Kent Tourist Attractions

Tourist Attraction Category	Tourist Attraction Type	Venue Name	Attraction Review	Hours of Operation	Price Range	Rating	Value Rating	Tourist Attraction Description
Land Tourist Attractions	Bird Watching	Fish River Lodge	Fish River Lodge Review	Morning to Evening	Free	Not Rated	Not Rated	Bald eagles, loons, songbirds; tour by boat, hike or drive; self-guided or fully guided tours. Inquire about package pricing.
Land Tourist Attractions	Cross Country Skiing	Fish River Lodge	Fish River Lodge Review	Morning to Evening	$20	Not Rated	Not Rated	Enjoy any of the numerous touring centers in Northern Aroostook County
Land Tourist Attractions	Dog Sledding	Fish River Lodge	Fish River Lodge Review	Morning to Evening	$150	Not Rated	Not Rated	Guided 1/2 day and full day trips with a team of racing huskies
								Black bear, whitetail deer, moose, upland birds, ducks.

Land Tourist Attractions	Hunting	Fish River Lodge	Fish River Lodge Review	Morning to Evening	Free	Not Rated	Not Rated	Self-guided, semi guided and fully guided. Inquire about package pricing.
Land Tourist Attractions	Mountain Biking	Fish River Lodge	Fish River Lodge Review	Morning to Evening	Free	Not Rated	Not Rated	Ride any of our hundreds of miles of dirt roads!
Land Tourist Attractions	Snowmobiling	Fish River Lodge	Fish River Lodge Review	24 Hours a Day	Free	Not Rated	Not Rated	Start here and ride anywhere, January - April. RENTALS available.

Rockland Tourist Attractions

Tourist Attraction Category	Tourist Attraction Type	Venue Name	Attraction Review	Hours of Operation	Price Range	Rating	Value Rating	Tourist Attraction Description
Land Tourist Attractions	Wine Tasting	Schooner Stephen Taber	Schooner Stephen Taber Review	Evening Only	Free	Not Rated	Not Rated	Wine tastings are included in the price for our wine trips.

Montana MT Tourist Attractions

Bozeman Tourist Attractions

Tourist Attraction Category	Tourist Attraction Type	Venue Name	Attraction Review	Hours of Operation	Price Range	Rating	Value Rating	Tourist Attraction Description
Land Tourist Attractions	Bird Watching	Bison Quest Wildlife and Bison Vacation Adventures	Bison Quest Wildlife and Bison Vacation Adventures Review	24 Hours a Day	$500	Not Rated	Not Rated	Experience a private bison & wildlife vacation in a cabin surrounded by a buffalo herd in the Montana wilderness, study wildlife and birdwatch alongside our internationally known biologists.

Water Tourist Attractions

Beaches	Dinner Cruises	River Cruises	Swimming Pools
Boat Rides	Fishing	Sailing	Water Parks
Body Surfing	Jet Skiing	Scuba Diving	Water Skiing
Crabbing	Kayaking	Snorkeling	Whale Watching
Deep Sea Fishing	Rafting	Surfing	Wind Surfing

Air Tourist Attractions

Airplane Rides	Hang Gliding	Parasailing
Ballooning	Helicopter Rides	Skydiving

Entertainment

Broadway Plays	Concerts	Movies
Comedy Clubs	Dinner Theaters	Theaters

Spectator Sports

American Football	Boxing	Golf	Tennis
Baseball	Bullfighting	Hockey	Weight Lifting
Basketball	Car Racing	Horse Racing	
BMX Racing	Cricket	Motorcycle Racing	
Bowling	Cycling	Soccer European Football	

Chapter–11

Facilities and Amenities

Tourist facilities are establishments which provide services within an area e.g. serviced accommodation, pubs, restaurants, cafes, cinemas/theatres, country clubs, garden centres, craft centres, museums and art galleries and studios where the prime function is sales, historic churches (only if open during the week), sports facilities (including swimming pools, motor sports courses, riding centres, bowling alleys and greens, golf facilities and the like). In rural areas these will be signed from the nearest numbered A or B road or nearest associated signed community, whichever is the nearer. If the tourist facility falls within a designated urban area, it will only be signed from the nearest classified road and only if the facility has 30 or more car parking spaces for general public use. If the facility is a camping / caravan site, a copy of the site licence will be required with the application.

It should be noted that a qualifying facility with direct access onto a numbered A or B road or other classified road in an urban area will only qualify for a 'flag' sign adjacent to the facility i.e. at the entrance to the facility. The following 32 areas will be regarded as urban for the purposes of the above paragraph:

Bodmin, Bude, Camborne, Falmouth, Fowey, Hayle, Helston, Launceston, Lizard, Liskeard, Lostwithiel, Looe,

Mevagissey, Mullion, Newlyn, Newquay, Padstow, Penryn, Penzance, Pool, Porthleven, Redruth, St.Austell, St. Blazey / Par, St Buryan, St. Ives, St.Keverne, Saltash, Sennen, Torpoint, Truro, Wadebridge

The extent of the designated area is taken as the built up area generally covered by 30 / 40mph limits and not any administrative boundary. There is not a threshold of a minimum number of visitors to qualify for signing; however the attraction/facility must be open to the general public on a regular basis. It will help in determining a request for signing if appropriate promotional literature is included with each application. Where operators wish to replace old blue and white tourism signs, new applications will be required. It should be noted that existence of blue and white signs does not guarantee new tourism signs will be allowed at the same locations. Each application will be determined in accordance with the criteria above.

The following will not be considered as tourist destinations:

1. Vehicle sales and repair
2. Office supplies
3. Furniture sales
4. Industrial estates
5. Property sales
6. Sales of bulky goods which cannot easily be taken home by tourists
7. Supermarkets
8. Other businesses predominantly dependent on local custom.

Medical Tourism Facilities

We merely provide a listing. A decision to engage the services of any facility or personnel is one that should be made after considering all the factors, and consulting with your personal health care professionals. If you represent a medical tourism facility, send us your information and we'll give you a free listing in our searchable database, and/or inquire about promotional placement across this site. If you have experience as a medical tourist, please feel free to comment on your experience at a specific facility. We welcome your contribution. Others in the medical tourism community will benefit from your evaluation. While OnlineMedicalTourism.com does not recommend facilities, we do provide an avenue for grassroots participation in the review and evaluation.

Tourism Facilities Near Harare : Case Study

The lake is Harare's main water supply and the surrounding land was declared a national park shortly after construction was completed in 1952. The game park, currently home to some of the last white rhino in Zimbabwe, was opened in 1962. The invasion was reported on Friday (January 21) when a mob of about 150 people arrived without warning on Kumba Shiri resort, where the renowned Larvon Bird Gardens are situated. Larvon Bird Gardens has aviaries housing approximately 120 species of birds and, as well as being Zimbabwe's bird orphanage, is also an education centre.

The invaders, wearing Zanu-PF regalia, put their own padlocks on the gates and residents in the 30 homesteads on the property were prevented from leaving. They were also not allowed to arrange the removal of any of their movable property. All of the workers in the bird gardens were also locked in, as well as a number of visitors. Police from Marimba eventually arrived at Lake Chivero late Friday afternoon but no action has as yet been taken against the forced take-over.

All along the lake shore approximately 20 clubs and other tourist facilities with either freehold title or leasehold from

National Parks have been similarly invaded with their gates locked. Viv Baxter from Wingate went over by boat to check on the caretaker at Jacana Yacht Club, Des Fenner, who is blind. He was taken hostage and only managed to return after several hours.

On Saturday afternoon National Parks personnel came out but the invaders have so far been allowed to continue their program. The owners of the tourist facilities have been warned by the invaders that this is the start of a countrywide indigenisation campaign that will initially target all tourist resorts where white people are involved. Kumba Shiri resort is owned by a South African investor, Gary Stafford.

BIPPA with South Africa

On May 15 last year, South Africa and Zimbabwe finally ratified a Bilateral Investment Promotion and Protection Agreement (BIPPA) that was signed by Zimbabwe's Economic Planning Minister Elton Mangoma and South Africa's Trade Minister Rob Davies in Harare in November 2009.

"The purpose of the agreement is to stimulate individual business initiatives and increase prosperity in both countries through the creation of favorable conditions for investment by South African investors in Zimbabwe and Zimbabwean investors in South Africa," the ministry said in a statement.

Negotiations for the deal started in 2002 as South African companies - the largest African investors in Zimbabwe – required reassurance that President Mugabe's government would abide by international norms regarding property rights following the violent land invasions.

Aaron Mazvi, leader of the invasion, is district chairman of the war veterans in the Zvimba community west of Harare, President Mugabe's rural home. In Mazvi's memo of January 6, 2011 to Minister Herbert Murerwa on "the take-over of properties along the lower and upper reaches of Lake

Chivero", Mazvi states the following on behalf of the "Zvimba community at large": "... In view of the government requisite that blacks should be empowered through the attainment of 51 percent shareholdings in foreign funded operations, I do hereby propose that the clubs be occupied and redistributed amongst community members and some be reserved for Ministers, top government officials, senators, Members of Parliament, Chiefs and those in the hierarchy of traditional leadership."

Previous Invasions

Aaron Mazvi has played a leading role in violent farm invasions in the Mashonaland West area, including the property next door, RB Ranches, where he currently resides. The first farm invasion in Mashonaland took place in 2000 on Saffron Waldon farm close by. The murder of two well-known white farmers in the district occurred during the early years of the invasions, notably the high profile beating and then shooting of commercial farmer Terry Ford (51) on Gowrie farm at Norton in 2002.

Don Stewart, a 68-year-old dairy farmer from Norton, was beaten and burnt to death in November 2005. Several of the farms in the area were taken over by the Mugabe family. Numerous cases of violence against farm workers were also recorded. Although in many cases the perpetrators are known, there is no record of any having been convicted.

Landmark SADC Torture Ruling

This month, in a landmark ruling that exposed Harare's flagrant disregard for the rule of law, the Namibian-based SADC Tribunal ordered the Zimbabwean government to pay damages to nine torture victims who had successfully claimed compensation in the High Court of Zimbabwe. The government had neglected or refused to pay compensation to the victims. Commentators said the ruling could open the floodgates for other victims of armed forces brutality who have failed to get fair hearings in Zimbabwe's partisan courts.

Background Information

Lake Chivero Recreational Park—Lake Chivero Recreational Park was opened in 1962 and holds a variety of game, most of which had originally been brought in from Lake Kariba during the internationally acclaimed game rescue operation known as "Operation Noah".

Game includes rhinoceros, zebra, giraffe, wildebeest, kudu, eland, waterbuck, tsessebe, bush pig, porcupine, pangolin and ant bear. The park was originally known as Lake McIlwaine Recreational Park in memory of the late Sir Robert McIlwaine, a former judge of the High Court and founder of Zimbabwe's Soil and Water Conservation Movement.

A popular destination for local and international birdwatchers, Lake Chivero has a wide variety of bird life, including African open bills, barbets, bee-eaters, buzzards, coots, cormorants, hamerkops, jacanas, kingfishers, grey herons, darters, Goliath herons, fish eagles, glossy starlings and lilac-breasted rollers. Several of the kopjies (rocky outcrops) have San (Bushman) paintings on their sheltered surfaces.

Cholera—Despite Lake Chivero being Harare's main water supply source, it was reported in August 2007 that the Zimbabwe National Water Authority (ZINWA) had dumped raw sewage into the lake. Public clinics reported they were treating about 900 cases of diarrhoea daily. On 4 December 2008, the Zimbabwean government declared the cholera outbreak a national emergency and called for international assistance. In September 2010 it was reported that raw sewage was being pumped directly into the Mukuvisi River, a tributary of Lake Chivero, and the situation was described as a "health time bomb".

Tourism Amenities

As the officials and the district administration gear up for another Dasara, the nine-day cultural extravaganza, Deccan Herald looks into the basic amenities and facilities surrounding the key tourist places in the city and finds glaring problems that bring a bunch of woes for visitors, particularly when the town is chock-a-block with hordes of tourists for over days. All the tourist places, be it the palace, the zoo, the St Philomena Church, Chamundi hill, Sri Jayachamarajendra art gallery presents a bleak scenario when it comes to meeting decent basic requirements like drinking water facility and toilets and secondary needs like cloak room and waiting lounges.

Though, the palace has visitors throughout the year, except for inside the palace precincts, the surrounding area does not have a clean drinking water facility or a toilet facility. Similar is the case with the Jayachamarajendra art gallery at the Jaganmohana palace. The trust maintaining the gallery has constructed a public toilet, which is badly maintained.

Often, the visitors and the localities are seen using the vacant place in the Gun house premises near Amba Vilas Palace and within the compound walls of Jaganmohana palace for urinals. The surrounding of Zoo poses even more difficult problems for those waiting in the queue. They would have to wait to get inside the zoo to get drinking water and access to toilets.

The place surrounding the St Philomena's Church also does not fare any better. The filthy roads surrounding the famous church itself attract public and tourist criticism in the area.

Although the top of the hill near Chamundeshwari temple is presently haunted with similar woes, thanks to the JnNURM project. The hill shrine would soon be equipped with citizens' infrastructure centre and bus stand facility to cater to basic amenities for visitors. The worst part of the scenario is all major commercial streets or the by-lanes do not have well maintained clean public toilets.

And, where they exist, people try to avoid them due to its unhygienic and filthy nature. When contacted, officials reason non - availability space in the prime localities or important roads in the town. The public also have a responsibility in keeping their city clean and maintain hygienic surroundings, an official told Deccan Herald.

Mahesh Kumar, a filmmaker who concentrates on making short documentaries on historical and tourist places says the city lacks a dedicated transport circuit connecting various tourist places. Forget running such vehicles throughout the year, such a facility is non-existent even during peak of the tourist season like Dasara and summer vacations, he says.

Local Facilitys and Tourist Information

Evron the main town, is about 7 km away and has a wondeful market each week on a Thursday providiving a real taste of France. It also boasts a magnificant basilica with good supermarkets, shops and a mainline train station. There is also a good tourist information office here and staff are always helpful.

Evron boasts a lidl, Aldi, Intermarchie and a super U. Intermarche is the eqivalent of Tesco. Whereas Super U is the equivalent of Sainsburys where as lidl and Aldi are the same as back home in England.

Gué de Sell

Also within walking distance but a little further is the Gue de Selle at Mesengers where there is a large lake with man made beach, five star resturant, hotel, small cafe, boats, picnic area and fishing. Large events are held hear each year which including cross country eqestrian tournaments. Come and discover a wide variety of safe sporting and water based activitys. Also available, children's playgrounds and fast food and restaurants. Which is a convinient five minute drive from the property.

Jublains

A place of great history. Come and be amazed by the facinating archaelogical finds.

Enjoy a leasurly stroal around a unique roman aphitheatre. Indulge yourself by taking a walk back in time by exploring the roman fort and let your imagination run wild, then gaze in awe at the roman temple. The museum of archaeology brings the roman city to life with videos and displays of archaelogical finds. Explore the roman baths and other places of intrest in the city with audio guides.

The Caves of Saulges

Come and dicover the magic and splendour of an underground world sculpted by time. Skillful lighting exposes the rocky walls and creates an exqusite atmosphere. We advise sensible shoes and jumpers as the arey of caves can be cold and slipy under foot. All tourists are guided through the caves in groups by profeshional and well trained staff. We warn you that only one cave allows for children. However there is a nice array of nature walks for the family.

The Tatin Museum

This is a magical place where the Overflowing imagination of an exceptionally talented artist is celibrated in a museum in the form of a palace. Houing strang and facinating paintings Inside and a variety of sculptures in the museums grounds.

You can also get guided tours in english. There is a small gift shop and the curators are always willing to answer questions.

Mayenne

Mayenne is a small town which sits astride the Mayenne river in the north of Mayenne department. It is on an east-west line between Le Mans and Rennes, south of Caen and north of Angers. To find the town's first distinguishing feature, you don't even need to visit, just look on a map. This is the only town in France which has the same name as the river and the department! This interesting fact, as you can imagine, leads to a fair amount of confusion.

The Loire Valley

The Loire Valley is found south of Paris, in the center of France. The valley from Sully-sur-Loire to Chalonne is listed as a French world heritage site by UNESCO. The Loire Valley falls into two French departments - The Centre and Pays de la Loire.

Le Mans

Le Mans is located on the Sarthe River. Traditionally the capital of the province of Maine, it is now the *prefecture* (capital) of the Sarthe *departement,* and is furthermore the seat of the Roman Catholic diocese of Le Mans. Its inhabitants are called *Manceaux* and *Mancelles*. It has been host to the famous 24 Hours of Le Mans sports car race since 1923.

Villaines la Juhel

The town of Villaines-la-Juhel was not created by chance. Its position on a strategic Roman way which enabled it to develop into the city which we know today. Its size confers a position of a town of the third rank on a departmental scale, at the demographic and administrative level. Villaines-la-Juhel is a relatively insulated rural pole and depends on other administrative divisions.

Villaines-la-Juhel counts 3180 inhabitants without double accounts. The commune covers 29 km^2 and has an average density of 110 habitants/km^2. It is the eleventh commune and the ninth most populated agglomeration department of Mayenne. It is located in the North-eastern part of Mayenne, with 56 kilometers of the Prefecture of the department, i.e. Laval. Its position, with the variation of the main roads, the great agglomerations, and the shoed network makes of Villaines-la-Juhel, a central pole for all this part of the department.

Saint Suzanne

In the middle of the Sarthe and the Mayenne, St Suzanne dominates the medieval town walls of the river Erve. Its dungeon, castle, old houses and its museum represent the richness of its history. The site is a paradise for hikers with more than

100 km of hiking trails, equestrian and mountain biking. At Sainte-Suzanne there are surrounding Numerous celebrations, medieval chivalry and performances for children and adults relive the life of the Middle Ages.

Sille le Guillaume

A large lake where many water sports are available. There is also a man made beach for that day at the sea side . The lake has several snack bars and restaurants in the surrounding woodland. Forest walks, cycle paths and picnic areas can all be found here.

St Leonard des Bois

A large Village with Bars and all outdoor sports and natural beauty.

Lassay-les-Châteaux

Lassay-les-Châteaux is a charming little town of character in the Mayenne.

You will discover the magnificent 15th century castle, still intact, but also the castle of Bois Thibault and the ruins of Wood Frou. Wandering the streets, you can admire beautiful houses of the 17th and 18th centuries. The area around Le Chataignier is beautiful and within walking distance of the farm is the medieval chapel of Motague, high on the hill, giving panaramic views of the surrounding countryside, with many events being held there during the summer months from half marathons to cultural events such as mime and music festivals.

CHAPTER–12

THE ACCESSIBILITY

Accessibility in tourism is how easy it is for the tourist to access or get to the desired destination. Accessibility refers to the ease or difficulty of taking advantage of an opportunity. The concept is commonly used in a spatial context in regards to the physical distance between a user and a tourism facility, that distance being measured in a straight line or along a route, by travel time, or by cost measured in monetary terms, or even in the degree of fatigue that is involved in overcoming the friction of distance. Maps may be drawn to display visually the travel times to a destination using isochrones (lines of equal travel time), with the lines generally extending outwards along major transportation corridors. However, there may be considerable differences between accessibility as determined by such measures and what is being perceived by potential tourists, and they may trade off travel time for money by substituting faster but more expensive transportation modes.

At a regional level, statistical methods have been used to assess the interaction of demand and supply for a particular resource at any point to calculate the potential, or accessibility, of that point. This concept has been used widely in transportation studies and marketing (Smith 1983). Changes in accessibility have major implications for tourism. Thus, for example, extensions of airline networks, frequency of flights and sizes of planes have greatly increased long-haul travel and the accessibility of distant locations. However, improved accessibility does not always stimulate tourism businesses. For example, Lundgren (1983) has shown how improvements in road transportation have allowed individuals to travel farther more quickly, thereby turning overnight into day-trip destinations and undermining the market for small accommodation establishments in intermediate locations. More generally, accessibility may be influenced by factors other than proximity, for example price, membership status and licensing regulations. Thus, even though a potential user may be very close to an opportunity, use may be prevented by barriers other than distance.

The ease of approach of a location from other locations, one of the prime factors which, together with its attractions and amenities (the three As), determine how important an area may be as a tourism destination. In tourism, accessibility is a function of distance from centres of population, which constitute tourist markets, and of external transport, which enables a destination to be reached. It is measured in terms of distance travelled, the time taken or the cost involved.

Accessibility and Equalities Act

The Equality Act 2010 came into effect on October 1st 2010 and has replaced existing anti-discrimination laws with a single Act. As providers of goods and services, tourism businesses have obligations under the Equality Act 2010. The Act has simplified the law, removing inconsistencies and making it easier for people to understand and comply with it. It also strengthened the law in important ways to help tackle discrimination and inequality.

Tourism providers should treat everyone accessing their goods, facilities or services fairly, regardless of their age, gender, race, sexual orientation, disability, gender reassignment, religion or belief, and guard against making assumptions about the characteristics of individuals. More advice can be found in the Summary guide for businesses who sell goods and services.

Who is Protected?

Equality legislation prohibits service providers from discriminating against or harassing customers or potential customers on the following grounds - called "protected characteristics":

1. Age
2. Disability
3. Gender
4. Gender identity
5. Pregnancy and maternity
6. Marriage and civil partnership
7. Race
8. Religion and belief
9. Sexual orientation

What is Discrimination?

Discrimination is not simply unfairness. The key is to provide the same service to all visitors which is sensitive to difference. Less favourable treatment happens when a service provider, on one of the grounds described above:

1. Refuses or deliberately fails to provide a service;
2. Provides a service of a lower standard or quality;
3. Offers a service on worse terms,

which it provides to members of the public or a section of the public. The most obvious form of discrimination occurs when a service provider refuses to serve a person or provides a lower standard of service because of a particular characteristic of a protected group. It applies to all organisations that provide a service to the public and anyone who sells goods or provides facilities, whether or not a charge is made for them.

It's about all businesses:

1. Being welcoming to all
2. Thinking through the visitor's experience in all its aspects to meet their needs
3. Thinking about universal design wherever possible to make services usable by all
4. Ensuring Poole's tourism product reflects world class modern standards of service, customer care and a welcoming environment

The following information concerns obligations with regard to disability only.

Disabled people must not be treated less favourably than others because they are disabled. Businesses also have an obligation to make reasonable adjustments to help disabled people access their goods, facilities and services. The Act makes significant changes in this area, introducing the principle of indirect disability discrimination and clarifying the three requirements for making reasonable adjustments and the point at which the duty to make reasonable adjustments is triggered.

The Act also introduces a new form of discrimination known as discrimination arising from disability. This occurs when a disabled person is treated unfavourably because of something connected to their disability.

Obligations

The law protects anyone who has, or has had, a disability; people who are mistakenly thought to be disabled; people who are linked or associated with a disabled person.

Direct Discrimination - must not treat someone less favourably because of the disability itself.

Discrimination arising from disability (NEW) - must not treat someone less favourably because of something connected with their disability e.g. refusing someone with incontinence.

Can Non-compliance be Justified?

Treatment can be justified and will be lawful if it can be shown that it is intended to meet a legitimate objective in a fair, balanced and reasonable way. This means that a service provider must strike a careful balance between the negative impact of a provision on the disabled person and any lawful reason for applying it.

Also, discrimination arising from disability will not be unlawful if the service provider can show that it did not know, or could not be reasonably expected to know, that the person was disabled. This means that:

Service providers should take reasonable steps to find out whether someone is disabled e.g. enquire as to whether anyone in the travelling party has any access needs.

Reasonable Adjustments

What is 'reasonable' will depend on a number of circumstances, including the cost of an adjustment.

The Equality Act 2010 requires that service providers must think ahead and take steps to address barriers that impede disabled people. Providers should not wait until a disabled person experiences difficulties using a service, as this may make it too late to make the necessary adjustment.

Make 'reasonable' changes to the way things are done - such as changing practices, policies or procedures where disabled people would be at a 'substantial disadvantage' e.g. amend a 'no dogs' policy.

Make 'reasonable' changes to the built environment - such as making changes to the structure of a building to improve access e.g. fitting handrails alongside steps.

Provide auxiliary aids and services - such as providing information in an accessible format, an induction loop for customers with hearing aids.

A service provider cannot legally justify failing to provide a reasonable adjustment. The only question is whether the adjustment is a 'reasonable' one to make.

Tourism Accessibility of Tasmania: Case Study

Tourism in Tasmania is increasing at a rapid rate as more and more people become aware of the beauties of our island at the bottom of Australia. As Education and Information Officer with Hearing Link Tasmania (a division of the Tasmanian Deaf Society), I have been regularly asked to try and improve the standards of service delivery with tour guides at our major sites. A regular complaint was that the tour guides don't enunciate well, they quite often talk to the scenery rather than the clients, or they talk too quickly. This is a common problem for not only the hearing impaired, but also for people for whom English is not their first language.

Many hearing impaired people say that when they participated in tours, they can't hear the commentary over the noise of other people. Quite often their hearing aids amplify not only the information they want to hear, but all the surrounding noise they didn't want to listen to (shuffling feet in gravel, side conversations, rustling papers, birds singing, wind in the trees, and passing traffic). This makes their tourism experience a frustrating and less than rewarding activity.

As an organisation that supports and assists people with hearing impairment, we worked with the Tasmanian Polytechnic – which provides tour guide training – to provide a short course in how to assist people with hearing impairment to get more out of tour presentations. During the course, we first play the students a tape of what hearing loss sounds like to people with hearing impairment. We advise them that rarely will clients tell them about their hearing loss and that they must look for the signs that the clients are unable to hear (leaning towards you, partners explaining what you said, looking elsewhere because they have lost interest etc)

We discuss the various aspects of hearing loss including the effects of tinnitus and Meniere's Syndrome and how hearing works for all of us. The groups and I then work on strategies for managing people with hearing loss. These include;

1. Always facing your audience when speaking
2. If you have to turn away to point out a feature, talk first, then turn and point
3. Speak a little more slowly than conversation speed and move your mouth to enunciate words as your audience is often lip reading.
4. Keep your sentences short and too the point.
5. Try to deal with one topic at a time only
6. Megaphones may make the sound louder, but also distort the sound, so avoid them where possible
7. Watch for signs of distraction and try to get those people engaged with the presentations by including them where you can. Remember that many people refuse to recognise or are embarrassed by their hearing loss, so you have to treat each situation with tact and diplomacy
8. If possible arrange to have voice directional FM system available to assist people with hearing aids to receive all of your presentation. If using an FM system, ensure clients have their hearing aid T switches turned on.
9. Try and get feedback on your presentations and be prepared to be flexible to your client's needs

The hearing loss and impairment training sessions have been running for the last two years in Tasmania and have been very well received by all the students. Longer term results will be analysed as we move further along with this program.

CHAPTER–13

STATISTICAL MEASUREMENT

The systematic measurement of tourism began not very long ago. The need was felt as the volume of tourist traffic began to reach significant proportions in the early years of the twentieth century. As the tourist movements grew tremendously, particularly in the last eight decades following the First World War, their measurements became very significant for various purposes. The frequency of occurrence of tourist movement in various countries engaged the attention of the statisticians and the social scientists in Europe, Switzerland, Italy, Austria and France which emerged clearly as tourist countries early in the century. Before the commencement of the World War I, Switzerland was a very popular destination for the rich and leisured class and was known to have received half a million foreign visitors annually. In the year 1929, foreign visitors to Austria were estimated at about two million, to Switzerland about one and a half million and to Italy about a million and a quarter. In Europe such statistics of tourism as did exist up to the First World War were mainly derived from government controls and enumeration records for health, safety and taxation and, in particular, for police and migration purposes. No distinction was made between tourists and other travellers. These statistics provided only some indication of the volume and value of tourist traffic.

Some other principal sources of quantitative data about tourism were the records of individual passenger transport and accommodation operators, the former giving numbers of travellers carried on particular routes and the latter giving numbers of travellers staying in hotels and similar accommodation establishments. These sources continue to be still utilised for quantitative data about tourism by many countries. In the absence of clear-cut definition of the term 'tourist', these sources rarely distinguished in any way between actual tourists and other travellers and also between different groups of tourists. These were thus of limited value in the assessment of the volume and the value of tourism. Tourism had not yet received recognition as an economic phenomenon and therefore not much efforts were made to systematically and scientifically measure it.

The post-World War I period witnessed a large-scale movement of tourists and tourism received recognition as a great economic phenomenon in the decade that followed. In the 1920s and early 1930s tourism came to be examined against the ' background of economic problems of most European countries. World War II, however, temporarily stopped the tourist movements.

Most of the European countries suffered tremendous economic losses as a result of the War. In the years immediately following the War, European economies were dominated by reconstruction and recovery, by balance-of-payment problems, and, in particular by the dollar gap. Tourism in these countries was seen as an important factor to the solution of various economic problems, especially the problems of the balance of payments.

The Data

It was however in the 1960s—the United Nations Development Decade—that much attention was focussed on the developing countries, their problems and solutions.

Various development plans were prepared by the experts in which tourism played a significant and a dominant role. The need arose for primary data on tourism to measure the tourist flows to particular destinations and of the tourist expenditure to provide a basis for planning the future development. Statistics thus became an essential tool of measurement of the tourist phenomenon. The emphasis, however, was on international tourism. Most of the statistics which were collected and analysed concerned the international tourist. During this period domestic tourism also gathered momentum. The governments realizing the importance of tourism gave a thought to its development. It was felt that both international and domestic tourism can contribute towards regional development within a country. Hence, in recent years, many countries have felt the need for the collection of tourist statistics of domestic tourist movements and expenditure and for the statistics related to particular destinations within a country.

Market research in recent years has brought about the need for quantified data in addition to the basic statistics about the movement and expenditure. A prospective tourist's choice of a particular destination or destinations is from a certain priority and related to his wants which could be physiological, psychological and/or sociological. These wants could be related to factors like recognition, a new learning experience, response from others, relaxation, etc. Marketing, decision-making and formulation of promotion strategies involve specialized knowledge and information of the buyer's likes and dislikes, preferences, etc. Therefore, it becomes necessary for a country to know about the potential tourist, his interests and needs and the level of the satisfaction for each of the interests. The characteristics of tourists and details of their behaviour are thus necessary for the purposes of marketing of the tourist product. Hence the need for obtaining quantified data became necessary.

The measurement of tourism phenomenon therefore is very vital. The importance of statistical measurement in tourism may be summarised as follows:

1. For evaluating the magnitude and significance of tourism to a particular tourist destination. The destination could be a country, a region or a district within a region. The data collected can be utilized to quantify the role and contribution of tourism to a country's economy.
2. For planning and development of physical facilities and for infrastructural requirements. It is not merely that statistics are useful to know the numbers of tourist arrivals for a series ' of consequent years to show whether tourist trade in any particular country is growing, stagnant or declining. It is important to know the other attributes like the mode of arrival, the kind of accommodation used, the amenities desired by the traveller, the length of stay, the amount that he spends, the purchases he makes, etc. All this information is necessary for tourism planning.
3. For marketing and promotion, it is essential to know the profile of tourists, both actual and potential. It is only after ascertaining the physiological, psychological and sociological wants of the visitors that an effective marketing campaign can be launched.
4. To know about the changes in tourist fashions. Regular returns of statistics help the countries to find out the flow of tourist traffic to various destinations. The flow will indicate whether a tourist patronises a beach holiday, winter resort, a historical place or any other place.

The Tourists

When we talk about measurement we must know as to what is to be measured. It is the 'tourist' who is the principal character in the phenomenon called tourism. Without his being around, the tourism phenomenon is meaningless. And when we talk about measurement, we mean measuring a 'tourist'. In other words, the tourist becomes the unit of measurement. The next question which comes up is, who is a tourist? How should a tourist be defined for the purposes of tourist statistics and for measuring the tourism phenomenon?

The origin of the word 'tourist' dates back to A.D. 1292. It has come from the word 'tour', a derivation of the Latin word *tornus,* meaning a tool for describing a circle or a turner's wheel. In the first half of the seventeenth century, the term was used for travelling from place to place, a journey, an excursion, a circuitous journey touching the principal parts of a country or region.

The *19th-century Dictionary* defines 'tourist' as a "person who travels for pleasure of travelling, out of curiosity, and because he has nothing better to do". The term 'tourist', the *Oxford English Dictionary* tells us, was used as early as the year 1800. According to the *Dictionnaire Universal,* the 'tourist' is a person who makes a journey for the sake of curiosity, for the fun of travelling; or just to tell others that he has travelled.

The term 'tourist' in the sense of a pleasure tour is, however, of recent origin. In the words of Jose Ignacio De Arrillaga, "tourism in its first period was considered as a sport or rather as a synthesis of automobiles, touring, cycling, camping, excursions and yachting. In the early nineteenth century, the term 'tourist' assumed a meaning of 'one who makes a tour or tours, especially one who does this for recreation or who travels for pleasure, object of interest, scenery or the like'."

Definition by League of Nations and the UN : All the above definitions of the term 'tourist' are of general nature and therefore could not serve the purpose of measurement.

It was, however, the League of Nations which did a pioneering work in defining the term for the purposes of statistical measurements. Realising the importance of collecting tourist statistics and of securing international compatibility, the Committee of Statistical Experts of the League of Nations in the year 1937 established the definition of the term 'tourist'. The League of Nations, with the concurrence of member countries, defined the term 'foreign tourist' as "any person visiting a country, other than that in which he usually resides, for a period of at least 24 hours."

The following persons were to be considered tourists within this definition:

1. Persons travelling for pleasure, for domestic reasons, for health, etc.
2. Persons travelling to meetings, or in a representative capacity of any kind (scientific, administrative diplomatic, religious, athletic, etc.).
3. Persons travelling for business purposes.
4. Persons arriving in the course of a sea cruise, even when they stay for less than 24 hours. (The latter should be reckoned as a separate group, disregarding if necessary their usual place of residence.)

The following categories were not to be regarded as tourists:

1. Persons arriving, with or without a contract of work, to take up an occupation or engage in any business activity in the country.
2. Persons coming to establish a residence in the country.
3. Students and young persons in boarding establishments or schools.
4. Residents in a frontier zone and persons domiciled in one country and working in an adjoining country.

5. Travellers passing through a country without stopping, even if the journey takes more than 24 hours. The above definition was confirmed by the United Nations in the year 1945 and it was stated that the 'tourist' was a person who stayed in a foreign country for more than 24 hours and less than six months for any non-immigrant purpose. The definition was adopted by many countries for the compilation of travel statistics.

European Travel Commission : The European Travel Commission (Etc.), the Organization for European Economic Cooperation (OEEC), and the International Union of Official Travel Organizations (IUOTO) were the agencies through which the first regular reporting was developed on the basis of the definition established by the Committee of Statistical Experts of the League of Nations. The European Travel Commission is a non-governmental body chiefly concerned with the promotion of American travel to Europe. The members of this commission are the national tourist organizations of some countries of Western Europe.

The IUOTO (later the World Tourism Organization), representing national tourist organizations on international basis, established the Study Commission on International Travel Statistics, and in 1947 began the publication of its *Digest of Tourist Statistics*. The document was a collection of national statistics of tourist arrivals and travel payments of some countries. In the year 1950 a permanent IUOTO Research Commission was established to study and recommend improvements in statistical methods. In December 1960 the Organization for Economic Cooperation and Development (OECD) was set up under a convention signed in Paris. It took over the work in tourism of its predecessor, the Organization for European Economic Cooperation. Up to the year 1963, the Tourism Committee of OECD recommended to its member countries the adoption of the definition of the term 'foreign tourist' established by the Committee of Statistical Experts of the League of Nations in 1937. Both the OECD and the IUOTO brought out many publications in the subsequent years concerning tourist statistics.

United Nations Rome Conference : In 1963, the United Nations Conference on International Travel and Tourism held in Rome considered a definition and recommended that it be studied by the United Nations Statistical Commission. A revised definition was prepared and adopted. The conference considered an overall definition of the term 'visitor' for statistical purposes and defines him as "any person visiting a country other than that in which he has his usual place of residence, for any reason other than following an occupation remunerated from within the country visited."

This definition covered:

1. Tourists, i.e., temporary visitors staying at least twenty-four hours in the country visited and the purpose of whose journey can be classified either as (a) leisure (recreation, holiday, health, study, religion, and sport) or (b) business, family, mission, meeting.
2. Excursionists, i.e., temporary visitors staying less than twenty-four hours in the country visited (including travellers on cruises).

The above definition excludes travellers who, in the legal sense, do not enter the country (e.g., air travellers who do not leave an airport's transit area).

The Expert Statistical Group on International Travel Statistics convened by the United Nations Statistical Commission recommended in 1967 that countries use the definition of 'visitor' proposed by the United Nations Conference on International Travel and Tourism in Rome in 1963. The group considered that it would be desirable to distinguish within the definition of visitor a separate class of visitors, who might be described as 'day visitors' or 'excursionists' defined as consisting of visitors on day excursions and other border-crossers for purposes other than employment, cruise passengers, and visitors in transit who do not stay overnight in accommodation provided within the country. The special characteristic of this category of visitors, distinguishing it from the main class of visitor, is that there is no overnight stay. In 1968 the United Nations Statistical Commission approved the Rome definition. These definitions are gradually receiving general acceptance. According to the studies published by World Tourism Organization, nearly 80 per cent of the countries use these definitions in the collection of international travel statistics.

The definition of 'foreign tourist' adopted by the Government of India's tourist department as per the recommendation of the United Nations Conference on International Travel and Tourism, Rome, 1963 is as follows:

"A foreign tourist is a person visiting India on a foreign passport, staying at least twenty-four hours in India and the purpose of whose journey can be classified under one of the following headings:

1. Leisure (recreation, holiday, health, study, religion and sport);
2. Business, family, mission, meeting."

The following categories are not regarded as foreign tourists in India:

1. Persons arriving, with or without a contract, to take up an occupation or engage in activities remunerated from within the country;
2. Persons coming to establish residence in the country;
3. 'Same-day visitors', i.e., temporary visitors staying less than twenty-four hours in the country (including travellers on cruises).

The following categories of travellers are not included in the data on foreign tourism:

1. Nationals of Nepal entering India through land routes along Indo-Nepal border,
2. All foreigners entering India from Bhutan by land; and
3. Children aged less than three years.

National Tourism

A distinction is drawn between domestic or internal and foreign or international tourism. In domestic tourism, people travel outside their normal domicile to certain other areas within the country as compared to travelling outside the boundaries of a country in international tourism. The basic difference between domestic and international tourism is that of jurisdiction of travel. The tourist activity of residents of a country within their own country, which does not cross the boundaries of the country, is thus described as internal or domestic tourism. Since the travel takes place within the limits of the boundaries of a country, the various travel formalities which are necessary in international tourism are not to be observed. The travel becomes an easy affair. The barriers of currency exchange, language, passport, visa, health documents, etc., are not to be faced by a domestic tourist. A tourist's own language serves as a medium of communication. The currency which they use in their everyday transactions continues to be the medium of exchange.

Presently there exists no generally accepted definition of the term 'domestic tourist'. The domestic tourist is generally regarded as a person travelling for a purpose other than exercising a gainful activity or settling at the place visited. The XXIII General Assembly of IUOTO held in Caracas, Venezuela in October 1973 recommended that a study should be carried out at the international level with a view to arriving at a standardized definition of domestic tourism. The following definition was put forward by IUOTO in 1974-75:

"For statistical purposes, the term 'domestic tourist' designates any person who travels within the country where he resides to a place other than his usual place of residence for at least twenty-four hours or one night, for a purpose other than exercising a gainful activity and which may be classified under one of the following headings:

1. leisure (recreation, holiday, health, study, religion and sport);
2. business, family, mission, meeting."

The above definition, however, was not adopted as an official definition but merely as a basis for discussion.

Three elements are common to the definitions normally in use. These elements are: (i) place of residence; (ii) geographical setting of travel; and (iii) duration of travel. With regard to place of residence most countries regard domestic tourism as travel by country's residents, within that country. The geographical setting is the national territory. Duration of travel is an important element in a number of definitions. The unit most often mentioned is the night spent at an accommodation establishment. By analogy with the accepted definition of 'international tourist', the domestic tourist is one who spends not less than twenty-four hours or makes an overnight stay away from his usual residence. Two further elements are common to most definitions of domestic tourism. These are (i) distance travelled and (ii) travel motivation.

With regard to distance travelled, some countries specify a minimum distance in their definitions. This may vary between 25 and 100 miles (between 40 and 160 kilometres approximately). The concept of travel motivation is considered important by most countries. The domestic tourist is generally considered as a person travelling for a purpose other than exercising a gainful activity at the place visited. Sometimes, domestic tourism is considered as including holiday or leisure travel only.

Measuring Problems

McEven has said that almost all international tourists have three actions in common: (i) they cross international frontiers, (ii) they exchange their own currency for foreign currency, and (iii) they spend time outside their own country, and this implies using some form of accommodation. It is possible to use these actions as methods for measuring international tourism, i.e., by enumerating arrivals at frontiers, by recording currency transactions and by recording number of nights in various types of accommodation units by the foreign visitors. None of these methods is, however, foolproof. Each method has its limitations in respect of recording and enumerating foreign visitors. Counting foreign visitor arrivals is the most usual and most widely adopted method.

The tourist statistics is basically concerned with arrivals and departures and more particularly with the former. In arriving at these figures, it is, as indicated above, concerned with events rather than individuals, and as far as these are concerned, half a dozen visits by the same person is counted as six separate events or six tourist arrivals. There are certain difficulties in the matter of counting. The main difficulty is perhaps the risk of double counting. Absolute figures of tourists visiting almost every country tend to be inflated because of double counting. For example, an Italian tourist on his way to holiday in Spain may travel by car for two days through France and on his return journey to Italy will also travel two days through France, hence his journey, i.e., his arrival in France is recorded twice. Another problem of statistical measurement in tourism arises from the difficulty of differentiating between tourists and other travellers and between them and the resident and working populations. In their movements and in their stay at various places at destinations it becomes difficult at times to distinguish between them and the residents and the working populations. Also regarding the use of transport to destinations, tourists may use public transport or use their own private transport. They normally enter various destinations without stopping and often without registering their arrival. They do so increasingly even when crossing many national frontiers. At the destination the tourists use a variety of accommodation ranging from hotels, pension apartments and guesthouses to friends' and relatives' homes. They eat in the same catering establishments and buy items for use and other services from the same sources from which these are bought by those who are not tourists.

It may, however, be stated that the various general problems of statistical measurements in tourism discussed above are to be encountered in countries having common borders. It is in these countries that distinction becomes difficult. A number of countries in Europe, Middle East, South America and South-East Asia encounter such problems of measurements.

Tourist Statistics

The tourist statistics is basically concerned with the figures of arrivals and departures, and more particularly the former. In addition to statistics of arrivals and departures, the statistics of tourist spendings during their stay at a destination have an important implication for the country's economy and on its balance of payments. Yet another type of tourist statistics is concerned with the information on the tourist himself. This information, which is very crucial for the purposes of tourism marketing and development, deals with various aspects of tourist behaviour and his characteristics. The main categories of the tourist statistics are therefore (i) volume, (ii) expenditure and (iii) characteristics.

Volume Statistics : The basic volume statistics consist of the number of tourists to a particular destination over a given period. The unit of period could be a month, six months or a year. Most of the countries, however, consider a year as the unit of the period. While counting, it is normally the number of arrivals or visits and not the number of tourists. This is because it is impracticable to allow for those who visit the same destination more than once in the same period. It is the events rather than individuals with which the basic statistics of volume are concerned. As already stated, half a dozen visits by the same person is counted as six separate events or six tourist arrivals. Thus 650 million tourist arrivals in the world in the year 1999 denote 650 million visits made by a somewhat smaller number of individual visitors. Length of stay is another main volume statistic. This is measured in terms of days or nights spent by a tourist at the destination and is normally expressed as the average length of stay. Thus the average length of stay of overseas tourists to India in the year 1998 was 28.6 days. This could be further subdivided in respect of nationals of different countries and regions. Thus the average duration of stay of nationals of South-East Asia in India in the year 1998 was 41.5 days compared to 28.0 days in case of nationals from Western Europe.

Statistics of numbers provide a general indication of the volume of tourist traffic to particular destinations. The statistics of length of stay, on the other hand, provide a general indication of the nature of the traffic, in particular of the extent of transit and terminal visitors and of their demand for overnight accommodation.

Data Sources for Travel and Tourism : The need for identifying the various data sources in the field of tourism has assumed a greater importance in the recent past. The data sources are very crucial as these help the practitioners of the tourism field to properly know at a glance the trends in tourism patterns, the markets and their requirements as also for planning and promotion. Over the past few decades there has been a multiplicity of these sources. The sources of information available today on travel and tourism have mushroomed and continue to grow with the growth in tourism activity all over the world.

Not only have the sources of information multiplied in volume, these have multiplied in range also. The wide range of data incorporate information of accommodation units, travel agencies and tour operations, transportations, recreation, research studies, books, periodical, journals, tourist statistics, regional tourism developments, employment, marketing trends and projections, etc. In fact, there is hardly a single tourism activity on which information is not available.

Together with the volume and range of information available on travel and tourism, the sources of information have also multiplied. There are a wide range of sources from where the information is made available. These include both private and government sources, travel agencies and tour operators, airlines companies, travel trade journals, reports and research studies. International organizations dealing with tourism and allied areas are yet another important source of supply of information. National tourist organizations of various countries contribute a great deal of material. Trade and professional associations are yet another source. Bibliographies, yearbooks, handbooks are other important sources of information.

The range, volume and the sources of information on travel and tourism are, however, not available at one place. There is a great need for development of a comprehensive list of volume, range and sources of information available on tourism so that it can be gainfully utilized by all concerned. Travel executives, officials in government and private sectors, international organizations, academicians as also the students of the subject require the above information and there is, therefore, an urgent need for providing the same to them. Such information can be used in not only analysing but also solving problems related to the travel industry.

Tables show the data required and their availability for obtaining a proper perspective of the tourism sector, for meeting the needs of development planning, for evolving marketing strategies, and for facilitating investment liaisons, respectively.

Data Required for Obtaining a Proper Perspective of Tourism Sector

Data Required	*Availability*
Number of tourist arrivals	(a) Data on foreign tourist arrivals are available on a regular basis from disembarkation cards (b) Data on domestic tourist traffic are not available from some of the regions and the data received from most others are unreliable
Tourist nights	Data on foreign tourists available on a regular basis
Outbound	(a) Total figures of citizens going abroad is available traffic from airports (b) Details of purpose of visit, destination, country, etc., are not available
Foreign exchange	Available on a regular basis earnings from tourism
Contribution to GDP	Derived from national income estimates
Employment generation	Derived from national income estimates and employment records

Data Required	*Availability*
Multiplier effect	Calculated on the basis of input-output tables
Regional impact	Not available
Social impact	No specific studies available
Ecological and environmental impact	No specific studies available

Data Required to Meet the Needs of Development Planning

Data Required	*Availability*
Demand	
Place-wise tourist visits and tourist	Periodical foreign tourist surveys provide details in respect of major centres. Partial information is available from the regional governments through monthly return-nights submitted by them.
Occupancy statistics of hotels	Response is good in the case of approved hotels. There is no system in the case of unapproved hotels.
Supply	
Hotel rooms	Details of approved hotels and rooms are available place-wise. Similar details in respect of unapproved and supplementary accommodation are not available in general.

Data Required	*Availability*
Restaurants	No details available
Shopping	No details available
Entertainment facilities	No details available
Tourist activities	No details available
International air seat capacity to a country	There is no regular flow of data on the subject from civil aviation authorities.

Data Required for Evolving Marketing Strategies

Data Required	*Availability*
Global trends	Available from WTO regularly
Country profiles	
Outbound traffic	Not available regularly
Preferred destinations	Available from WTO for certain nationalities
Economic situation	GDP figures are available from WTO
Political situation	Normally reported by the overseas tourist offices
Legislations, regulations	Overseas tourist offices usually report them and advisories
Market segments	Not much information available
Profile of tourists	
Age	In the case of tourists who visit the country details of (a) and (c) are available from disembarkation cards.

Data Required	*Availability*
Sex Occupation	Details of (a) to (c) are also available from periodical foreign tourist surveys.
Place of residence	No such details are available in the case of (a) to (b) except through PATA
Purpose of travel	Cooperative Market Research Studies and certain studies undertaken by the respective countries.
Travel habits Travel planning Choice of destination factor Motivations Perceptions Media affinity Reading habits	
Reactions of	Available from periodical foreign tourist surveys tourists to facilities
Activities of destinations	Not much being documented competing
Feedback/ evaluation	
Awareness created	Tourist offices abroad maintain certain basic information
Response received Departure rates	

Data Required to Facilitate Investment Decisions

Data Required	*Availability*
Locational details	
Availability of land, water electricity, etc.	Being compiled
Transport facilities	Being compiled
Incentives available	Being compiled
Profitability of existing units	Not available
Occupancy rates	Not available for most of the centres due to non-reporting of data
Taxation policies	Information is available in bits and pieces

The importance of statistical data on travel and tourism today is well recognised by all the concerned authorities responsible for policy planning and marketing and promotion of tourism. No organization can effort to neglect this vital source of information on which depends the accurate assessment of the sector and its role in the economic development of a country.

Survey Planning

Social research is becoming increasingly an important activity. It is extremely important for the agency which wants to undertake any research to understand the basic research procedures. The knowledge about the basic rudiments of careful and systematic inquiry is very essential for undertaking any research.

There are a number of steps or closely related activities involved in research. All these steps follow a prescribed sequence. However, all the steps need not follow a rigid sequence but may overlap as well. The steps in research are also very much interdependent. One step determines the nature of another. Every step of the research process is so wide that separate chapters can be written on them. However, only a brief account of the steps is given.

Formulation of the Problem : Formulation of the problem is one of the very important steps in research. We have to put a great deal of thought into the formulation of our questions if we hope to get anything out of an effort to answer them. In order to solve the problem, it has first to be carefully formulated. The more carefully the problem is formulated the more satisfactory is the solution we obtain. Before formulating a problem we have to first determine what a 'problem' is. The problem must be clearly defined as it should give guidance in the construction of research design. By allowing design considerations to influence problem definition, the researcher tends to limit his choice to those problems about which objective data can be readily obtained. Hence, we find that formulation of the problem is a very essential step of research.

Specifying Objectives of the Survey : The objectives of the survey must be clearly spelt out. This is very important and helps in achieving and measuring the results. Both general as well as specific objectives of the survey must be clearly defined. The objectives make it clear as to why we are conducting the research and what we are trying to get out of it. Where do we look for the objectives and how do we go about formulating them? In general, there are three sources to take into account before formulating objectives. These are (a) the research consumer, (b) the researcher and (c) those who will be affected by use of the research results. All pertinent objectives are the most important in order to know how to evaluate any potential solution to the problem. The objectives, however, should be simple and clear. They should be framed in a simple language.

Selecting a Survey Area and Survey Population : The particular area where the survey is to be undertaken must be carefully chosen. Great care should be taken before choosing an area. Many important factors such as importance, feasibility, personnel available for study, its use to community, organization, etc., must be taken into consideration. Regarding study population, it should be carefully selected. Obtaining information on results by observing or by questioning the entire group of people potentially affected would be an extremely difficult task. Therefore, a sample of population is to be selected. By observing or questioning only a fraction (sample of the group) the desired information can be obtained more economically, more quickly and accurately. But samples, whether random or stratified, should be selected properly without introduction of personal bias or other biases as to its size and representativeness.

Deciding the Nature and Scope of Survey : Yet another essential step of research is the decision regarding the nature and scope of the survey. The decision about the type of survey will also depend upon its purpose. There are different types of studies. Broadly, the surveys can be classified by (a) purpose and (b) approach used. Surveys of foreign tourism maybe divided into several types according to purpose and scope and according to where and when interviews take place. The survey may not, however, be classified according to some precise or rigid system. What is important is that they should be well designed and carefully done, whatever type they may be. It is also important that specific nature of the survey should be determined early, particularly when time and resources are limited.

Selecting Methods and Techniques : Great care is to be taken in the selection of methods and techniques of data collection. The findings of the survey will greatly depend on how scientifically methods have been selected. The methods by which data are to be collected or obtained must be devised after the problem has been formulated. Techniques are to be devised for collection of information. There are various methods of data collection, namely, interviewing, observation, questionnaires, projective techniques, examination of records, etc. All these methods have advantages and limitations. Selection of a particular type of method will also depend upon the type of survey for which data is to be collected.

Selection or Designing Survey Instrument : Selection of appropriate instrument for data collection is a fundamental step in a research project. This carries heavy implications for the entire study. Instrument must therefore be selected very carefully. Once it is decided as to which instrument will be used in the survey, the question of its designing or construction comes. While constructing the instruments care should be taken to see that it is simple, and not loaded and confusing. The questions should be so framed that the respondent may not have any difficulty in answering them. It should produce useful information. The questions should be clear and straightforward and easy to comprehend.

Pretesting and Revising Instruments : After the data-collection instruments have been framed, they must be pretested before they are used in the final study. Questions, which at first may seem simple and straightforward, may prove difficult to comprehend during trials. They may prove to be ambiguous or simply not productive of useful information. In addition, the categories may be inappropriate. To avoid all this it is essential to pretest the instruments and subsequently revise it for the final use. Pretesting the instrument's will ensure that they will collect the right type of information.

Data Collection : Data denote all the relevant materials, past and present, which serve as basis for study and analysis. The data must be carefully collected. Adequate care should be taken to see that they are collected honestly and consistently. They should be unbiased and free from errors.

They should be checked for completeness, comprehensibility and reliability. Such checking will prevent difficulty at later stages when the data are arranged. Care should also be taken to ensure that the timing of data collection is convenient to the respondent.

Analysis of Data : The collection of data, however, is only one important step in research. The data are to be analysed for meaningful interpretation. The amount of data collected may be huge and extremely varied. This has to be systematically arranged. The process of analysis includes: editing, classification and coding (placing each item in the appropriate category) and tabulating (counting the number of items in each category) and statistical computations. In order to save time at the later stages, it is necessary that the analysis be planned in detail before actual work on it is started. A simple basic outline of analysis should be prepared in advance.

Interpretation of Data : The data analysed are to be meaningfully interpreted. The interpretation of findings is interrelated with the analysis. Both are involved in the writing of survey report. Interpretation takes the results of analysis, makes inferences pertinent to the research questions studied, and draws conclusions about these questions. Interpretation of data should be done very carefully. Results of the survey greatly depend on this. Care should be taken to ensure that a major portion of the data analysed should be interpreted. It is advisable that a plan should be prepared beforehand as to the manner in which the data are to be interpreted.

Writing of the Report : Writing the report is the final step of research. The process of research becomes incomplete until the report has been written and distributed. The report should be written in a simple and meaningful language so that different consumers may not have difficulty in grasping its findings. It should also be brief and precise. At the end, a summary containing the essential points should be given.

The final report can be utilized in different ways. It can be useful for the guidance of the agency sponsoring the research in dealing with some practical problem. It may be useful for a wider audience with similar problem. Finally it may be of use to administrators in formulating policies.

CHAPTER–14

TOURISM PROMOTION

Tourism is one of the largest & important industry which is useful for the development of a nation. It occupies 11% of the world's GDP and may create 7 million new jobs by the year 2010. $595 billions have been generated by the international tourism industry in 2000.

Promotion is one of the four elements of marketing mix (product, price, promotion, distribution). It is the communication link between sellers and buyers for the purpose of influencing, informing, or persuading a potential buyer's purchasing decision.

The elements of the promotions mix are:

1. Personal Selling.
2. Sales Promotion.
3. Public Relations.
4. Direct Mail.
5. Trade Fairs and Exhibitions.
6. Advertising.
7. Sponsorship.

The elements of the promotions mix are integrated to form a coherent campaign. As with all forms of communication. The message from the marketer follows the 'communications process' as illustrated above. For example, a radio advert is made for a car manufacturer. The car manufacturer (sender) pays for a specific advert with contains a message specific to a target audience (encoding). It is transmitted during a set of commercials from a radio station (Message / media).

The message is decoded by a car radio (decoding) and the target consumer interprets the message (receiver). He or she might visit a dealership or seek further information from a web site (Response). The consumer might buy a car or express an interest or dislike (feedback). This information will inform future elements of an integrated promotional campaign. Perhaps a direct mail campaign would push the consumer to the point of purchase. Noise represent the thousand of marketing communications that a consumer is exposed to everyday, all competing for attention.

Personal Selling

The salesman sells goods and services at his shop or goes to the house of the buyer. This is a time-tested technique that helps the seller push his products and services in the targeted markets. His personality, features of the product and the brand name of the product that he tries to sell are the important factors that would win the customers for him. It is not an easy task by any norm. But we know many people who are successful sellers and on the top of the world, literally! They can sell ice to an Eskimo and combs to a bald man. Their communication abilities are superior to those of other departments of the firm. They are always mobile. They ,wear the finest of clothes and are suave, well-mannered and result oriented. They talk in terms of sales figures. They are the real gems of any organisation they work for. They work on their customers on the basis of the AIDA theory (Attention, Intention, desire and Purchase).

Sales Promotion

The seller uses displays and demonstrates the products and services, samples and point of purchase advertising. This tool requires PoP display material, quantity discounts, reduction in sales prices and freebies so that the prospective customers could be "hooked on" to the products and services of the firm. Shopkeepers (retailers) are the major conduits for supplying these promotional items and schemes to ultimate customers. Examples: Deepawali season sales, off-season sales, additional quantities at the same price, free welcome drinks during a tour, free airport-hotel-airport transfers, complementary stay for an additional night in a hotel, free garlic bread in holds before the product (food) is served, free bags from airlines, free wine bottles to frequent fliers etc are some of the prominent examples from various fields. The IA-Taj offer is also a sales promotion scheme under which, passengers can stay in any of the hotels of the Taj Group at an additional cost of *Rs 2,000.* Aishwarya Rai promotes Nakshatra Jewellery as its brand ambassador.

Advertising

This is a paid form of non-personal presentation and promotion of goods. It is done by an identified person or company. It motivates people to buy goods or services, or to accept (or reject) a point of view. Some exclusive and finely developed messages can be given to a large number of people at the same time. This exercise falls under the gamut of mass communication.' Its objective is to make people aware of the products or services they need. It also introduces new products and services. The chief aim of advertising is to create an interest in the products. So, the salesmen would find it easy to sell the products and services in the local, regional and global markets, if the advertising exercises were done with professional finesse. The firm can reach a large number of people at very low costs: The firm can increase the number of users-light, medium and heavy—of the product or service. It can also motivate or persuade the present buyers to increase their consumption levels. The tastes of consumers can be changed, albeit slowly through the introduction of new .products and services; for this purpose, advertising gimmicks play major roles in influencing the psyche of masses.

Publicity

It is a non-paid form of promotion. The sponsor of publicity is not a person or firm who gets the benefit of the same. However, publicity campaigns are being sponsored nowadays even by those who are desperate for such modes of promotion. Firms participate in seminars and conferences related to their respective trades. They advertise their products and services (at nominal costs to them) at such occasions. They also send their representatives abroad and try to get additional clients for their products and services. Naturally, these efforts cost a lot. But some others do not. Example: A political candidate may be supported by a firm in an election campaign. The exercise is a ploy of this firm to promote its products and services. The candidate also feels pleased because he is getting the political support of a firm. Issuing press statements is also a part of publicity campaigns. Such efforts do not cost a penny to the firm. In this section, we shall concentrate on the major component of promotion-advertising.

Sale of Product or Service based Division

We can either sell the product or we can sell a good image of OUI: company through advertising. So, we have 2 classifications in this context.

Product : Promot on Product : This is done to increase the sale of a product. It can be done by manufacturers of consumer or industrial products. It can be done for a particular brand as well. **Examples:** Sansui's offers in newspaper advertisements. Pringle *(Special Privilege Offer).*

Service : Promotion of Service : Firms that give services indulge in this type of advertising efforts. Their objective is to attract customers towards their services. **Example:** Airtel *(Free incoming calls to cellular phones).* Advertisements of travel agencies of various tour packages.

Concept : Promotion of Concept : The firm tries to communicate to the targeted audience that the concept would help them achieve better standards of living. Or, they would get better results as a result of acceptance of the concept promoted by the firm. But the insinuations are totally commercial in nature. **Example:** Advertisements of small business houses, persuading targeted readers to surf through the Net and earn money. In fact, these firms would also earn money when these Net surfers would work for them.

Societal Concept

Such advertisements are issued to inform the society about issues of great importance. The objective is not commercial- exploitation but societal transformation. Example: Advertisements of the government against dowry, AIDS, family planning (e.g, vasectomy), neighbourhood watch scheme etc.

Institutional : Promoting for Changing the Brand Image as a Society-friendly Entity: Its other name is Corporate Advertising. In these exercises, there is no overt reference to the product manufactured by the firm. The stress is on building the image of the firm so that it is remembered as a great corporate player. Many experts opine that institutional advertising is synonymous with public relations advertising. In the times of crises, this type of advertising may be to mend fences and give the viewpoint of the firm in a lucid manner. At other times, its objective may be to build trust attract talent or establish/inform the contribution of the firm towards the country, society or neighbourhood. Example: Advertisements of Sahara in newspapers and Sahara TV channel on the issue of national integration.

Advocacy : Promotion of Changing Attitudes : This type of advertising effort is useful in changing the thoughts of the targeted audience. The advertiser wants to achieve an objective when he tries to change the attitude of the targeted audience. The group of people who advertise such typical messages are not necessarily united under organisations. The cause may be too pious to use highly structured organisations. Examples: Advertisements of **Safal** products in favour of vegetarianism. Advertising campaigns of political parties (e.g, Congress: *Elect a Government That Works).*

Promotion of the People

Normally, political parties promote their candidates during election campaigns and election rallies. Corporate firms may also undertake such exercises, if the persons in question are very much important for the firm. Example: Arrival of a foreign dignitary in India and subsequent displays of his photographs or portraits and life-size cut-outs throughout the city.

Media for Advertisement based Division

There are 7 categories in this broad classification, as follows :-

Audio Promotion

It is done over radio and PA systems and through auto-rickshaw promotions, four-wheeler promotions etc.

Visual Promotion through Visual Displays : It is done through PoP displays, catalogues (without text), leaflets (without text), cloth banners, brochures (without text), electronic hoardings, simple hoardings, running hoardings etc.

Audio-visual Promotion through TV, Cinema : It is done through cinema slides, movies, video clips, TV advertisements, cable TV advertisements and campaigns on CCTV systems.

Written Display : It is done through letters, fax messages, ieaflets (with text), brochures (with text) articles and documents, space marketing features (in newspapers) etc.

Internet Promotion through Websites : The world wide web is used extensively to promote products and services of all genres. Read *Effective Business Communication* by A Kumar in this context. Various web sites of individuals and firms are, in fact, messengers of these firms that have been telling people from thew skies to buy their products, services and thoughts.

Verbal Promotion through Voice Gestures : Verbal tools are used to advertise thoughts, products and services during conferences, seminars and group discussion sessions.

Aims of Advertising : The following objectives of advertising have become relevant in the context of operations of the business and non-business firms in the new millennium :-

The Information

To introduce new products in old markets.

To introduce old products in new (or foreign) markets.

To introduce new versions of old products.

To give vital facts and data related to health, family planning, inoculation campaigns, elections etc.

To combat competition in an effective manner.

To convert light users into medium users and medium users into heavy users.

To increase sales during off-seasons.

To effect sales during peak seasons.

Cognitive Dissonance

To reduce or eliminate cognitive dissonance from the minds of the customers who have Purchased the products and services of the firm.

To remind the customers that their purchase decisions were the best ones.

To sell more to the same set of customers by making them "feel good" after reducing their post-purchase cognitive dissonance.

To obtain dealers' support.

To build a positive business image in the minds of the public at large.

To secure leads for sales people.

To increase the number of units purchased.

To maintain brand loyalty among the existing set of customers.

Brand Image

To create a brand image through corporate advertisements.

To sustain brand image through advertisements in print and audio-visual media.

Society Oriented Image

To inform the society that vital community issues are being -addressed.

To give support to issues related to ecology and environment.

To create awareness among the masses about issues like environment protection, pollution control, health and education.

Tourism World and Role of Advertising

Advertising is an integral part of our social and economic systems. It is a powerful technique of sales promotion and has been doing wonders in the domain of distribution because it is quite capable of influencing the consumption patterns of customers. It also affects the processes of production and distribution. That is why, it is said that advertising is the Archimedian lever that motivates the world of commerce and industry.

In this volume, we are chiefly concerned with advertising efforts of the tourism industry. The role of advertising in the tourism world can be analysed with 5 distinct players of its gamut, namely, manufacturers; middlemen, sales force, consumers and the society.

Chapter–15

Economic and Social Significance

The need to promote the value of an industry sector should be paramount in the strategic direction of any sustainable industry. Tourism is no different.

It is important that the industry focuses on social and environmental as well as economic benefits of tourism. This is not to suggest that economic considerations are mutually exclusive from those of social cohesion and the environment. In fact, sustainable economic returns can only be achieved through factoring in strategies that take all three elements into account.

The emphasis on tourism will increase due to:

1. The continuing economic shift from traditional to service based industries;
2. Greater focus caused by terrorism and airline crises in 2001 that highlighted the depth of tourism influence on economies and communities;
3. Concentration on industries with capacity to increase export earnings; and
4. Tourism being one of the few established industry sectors projected to maintain significant growth over a long period.

Tourism is one of Australia's largest industries. It accounts for $48.7 billion or 8.6% of Australia's Gross Domestic Product. This represents a greater contribution than the agriculture or communication services sectors. For Victoria, tourism is worth $8.5 billion to the State's economy, contributing 5.2% to Victoria's Gross State Product.

As part of the international economy, tourism is a major force as it generates 11.2% of Australia's total export earnings, more than traditional exports such as coal, iron and steel products. It is forecast that tourism's export growth rate will outperform all key sectors by 2004-2005. Tourism is an important economic driver. In Victoria, $11 billion was spent by domestic and international visitors in 1998.

Revised forecasts from the Tourism Forecasting Council predict international visitor arrivals to Australia will reach 9.4 million by the year 2010. International visitors are forecast to grow at an average annual rate of 6.6% over the next 10 years.

The Australian economy is fundamentally shifting from primary industry to a service and knowledge base. The total number of jobs increased by 17.3% between 1986 and 1996, but employment in agriculture (11%) and mining (6%) declined. Farming is losing its position as the primary industry of most rural economies. Decreasing farm profitability and labour efficiencies from agricultural technology and mechanisation have changed rural employment.

Tourism can promote and facilitate economic activity that supports aspects of regional life. For example, farm stays, cellar doors and the purchase of local produce support agriculture, while the purchase of other products supports local retail and industry. Tourism spending also has a multiplier effect in the local economy as it is spent and re-spent by employers and employees.

Tourism may generate income for local government in the form of rates and levies or as a result of patronage of local government owned attractions and services. This income contributes to the quality and quantity of local services and facilities provided for the benefit of both residents and visitors.

Economic Impact of Tourism

The service economy is driving growth in most OECD countries. It represents a large part of economic activity and its importance continues to grow. Tourism, a large, complex and fragmented industry which is still very difficult to define and measure, is a key component of the service economy (30% of international trade in services in the OECD area). In terms of revenue, OECD countries generate about 70% of world tourism activity. Tourism, which has expanded dramatically over the past 30 years, looks set to continue growing as societies become more mobile and prosperous.

Obtaining better information on services, the least developed side of statistics, is an important challenge for statistical agencies and a necessity for political analysis. Measuring tourism is part of a wider move to improve our knowledge of how economies work, what they produce and what changes occur over time. It is no longer enough to measure physical flows (arrivals and overnight stays) and monetary data (revenue and expenditure relating to international tourism).

In the early 1980s, the OECD began work to set up a model acceptable at international level which gave rise to the OECD Tourism Economic Accounts, which measure certain socio-economic aspects of tourism. While developing this tool, the OECD produced a more precise definition of tourism, visitors and tourist expenditure [Note: OECD (1996), OECD Tourism Statistics - Design and Application for Policy].

Despite its economic importance, governments, especially in developed economies, still do not adequately recognise tourism. For this reason, the OECD has developed and recently approved the OECD Guidelines for a Tourism Satellite Account and an Employment Module. These integrated statistical tools aim to measure the economic aspects of tourism (value added, jobs, revenue, investment, profits) in order to provide a more convincing demonstration of this activity's economic significance.

Furthermore, together with the United Nations, the World Tourism Organization and the European Commission (Eurostat), the OECD has developed a "UN-WTO-OECD-EUROSTAT Tourism Satellite Account: Recommended Methodological Framework", approved by the 25-member United Nations Statistical Commission on 1 March 2000.

Other work undertaken in this area includes statistical research. OECD and Eurostat regularly organise international forums on tourism statistics to share ideas, experiences and concepts with member and non-members countries, the scientific community and the tourism industry. The United Kingdom, with the support of Eurostat and the OECD, organised the 5th International Forum on Tourism Statistics (Glasgow, 20-23 June 2000). Similar forums have been organised in Vienna (1994), in Venice (1995), in Sintra (1996) and in Copenhagen (1998).

Social Value of Tourism

Tourism activity offers social benefits to Victoria, such as:

1. Generating community cohesiveness through the development of social capital.
2. Facilitating regional pride and local community involvement.
3. Contributing to the revival of regional towns.

Tourism is a driving force behind the renewal of regional centres:

Tourism contributes to the development of regional communities through building partnerships between local people, local organisations and local businesses. By being innovative and embracing tourism, Beechworth has transformed from a contracting community based on institutional employment, to a major tourism centre with a growing population and employment opportunity and diversity.

Beechworth's focus on heritage tourism has enabled the preservation and conservation of unique heritage streetscape. It now has a national reputation for heritage tourism, special events, arts and crafts, farm tourism and the bed and breakfast industry.

Source: Small Town Renewal: change the future of your community, 2001, Rural Industries Research and Development Corporation

Events play a major role in regional and state economic and social development:

Port Fairy Folk Festival is one of the largest folk festivals in Australia. The festival has funded a wide range of community facilities within the Shire of Moyne, making the festival committee an influential economic player in the local community. The 1998 Port Fairy Folk Festival had an economic impact of $1.8 million to the region, the equivalent of 54 effective full time jobs.

Source: Port Fairy Folk Festival - Economic Impact Study, 1998, Pricewaterhousecoopers

Tourism is a labour intensive industry that provides many full-time and part-time employment opportunities across a range of skill areas. Being relatively decentralised, it provides jobs that keep people in regional areas with flow-on benefits for community life and economic stability.

Environmental Sustainability

The tourism industry as a large, diverse and growing sector is an integral part of the State's economy and has an important role in achieving environmental sustainability. It is argued that meeting this sustainability challenge is essential for the future viability of tourism. This is because more than any other industry, tourism possesses a natural synergy with the concept.

In Victoria, the environment, in particular the natural environment, is one of the State's major tourist attractions. Research has established that the State's magnificent scenic areas are key interests for visitors. This research clearly establishes that international and domestic visitors regard the State's clean, unspoilt natural environment as one of the primary motivators for a visit to Victoria.

The interdependence of tourism on the quality of the environment places it in a very special position in terms of environmental sustainability. Unlike the situation with most industries, concern for the environment should not be seen simply as a cost. Indeed, if sustainably managed, tourism can produce great benefits for visitors, residents and the environment. In fact, travel and tourism were identified in Agenda 21 as one of the few industries that has the potential to make a positive contribution to a healthier planet. Agenda 21 is a program of action adopted by 182 governments at the 1992 United Nations Conference on Environment and Development (UNCED) Earth Summit.

Environmental Benefits of Tourism Include:

1. The opportunity to communicate the value of natural and built heritage and of cultural inheritance to residents;
2. Enhancement of the natural and built environment to meet rising quality standards necessary to sustain modern tourism;

3. Providing the incentive for environmental enhancement or rehabilitation of areas such as town/city centres and old industrial sites, including the creation of employment in these areas;
4. Cost savings to individual tourism businesses through the adoption of waste and energy minimisation practices;
5. Protecting and creating economic value for resources which otherwise have no perceived value to residents, or represent a cost rather than a benefit; and
6. Raising awareness of environmental issues and stimulating tourists to advocate for conservation through education and interpretation. Environmental appreciation can in turn enhance visitor enjoyment.

Increasing Access to Tourism

The industry has both an economic and social interest in ensuring that travel is available to all members of the community. More than 3.6 million people in Australia have a disability, or almost 19% of the population. With Australia's population ageing rapidly this figure is expected to increase within the next decade.

In 1997, it was estimated that the domestic overnight market for disabled visitors generated expenditure of about $472 million Australia-wide. Given the international attention of such high profile events as the Paralympics 2000 and the increased number of disabled visitors from overseas, the size of this potential market becomes apparent.

Apart from it making good business sense to better cater for, and actively market to this significantly large group of consumers, the industry has a social responsibility to increase access for people with a disability. Tourism Victoria, together with the State's tourism industry, has a legal responsibility under the Disability Discrimination Act 1992 (Comm.) and relevant state legislation not to discriminate against people with a disability.

Multiculturalism

Australians represent more than 145 different cultural and linguistic groups. Victoria, in particular, has the opportunity to capitalise on the diversity of cuisine and experiences these groups provide to the State. Embracing different cultures not only highlights the importance of their heritage, it provides the Victorian community with an opportunity to become aware and involved with different ethnic groups.

The cultural and historical connections between Great Britain and Australia have helped facilitate more travel between the two nations. Established networks exist between Australia's large immigrant communities and source nations. There is an opportunity to develop further ties with nations such as Italy, Greece, China and other Asian countries.

A significant number of immigrant communities have been established across Victoria's regions. There are Italian, Greek, Chinese, Turkish and Middle Eastern associations and clubs in regional Victoria. Effective communication with these groups could have an incremental benefit in both the Visiting Friends and Relatives and Education markets.

Aboriginal

International visitors have a great interest in Aboriginal culture, according to Australian Tourist Commission research. While Victoria may not have the depth and breadth of Aboriginal tourism products available in other regions of Australia, it has a rich and diverse Aboriginal culture.

The strength of Victoria's emerging Aboriginal tourism segment focused on unique heritage and non-stereotypical contemporary experiences, offers a great opportunity for Aboriginal communities and the tourism industry.

The value of tourism for the Aboriginal community is twofold:

1. It provides a vehicle to facilitate pride among the Aboriginal community in the intrinsic culture and history of Aboriginal life; and
2. Assists in a greater understanding of Aboriginal culture by non-Aboriginals.

Issues

There are a number of issues and barriers that have influenced the ability to sell the value of tourism to government, the business sector and general community. This includes the ability to define the tourism industry and its influence on other sectors such as retail.

The above point is exacerbated by an industry primarily consisting of small to medium sized businesses. Without a combined industry voice and large influential businesses, it makes it very difficult to have tourism placed on government and private sector agendas. Tourism has therefore struggled to gain recognition in public policy priorities.

Tourism has significant impact and potential for job creation, export earnings, and social cohesion, but traditional economic and social development strategies have failed to understand and identify these opportunities.

Local government is showing a greater propensity to embrace tourism. However this is not consistent across the board and needs to be enhanced.

The key challenge is for tourism businesses in all parts of the industry to adopt ecologically sustainable practices in their day-to-day operation. Businesses, particularly small business must increase their commitment to safeguarding the environment as it is the basis for much of their trade. Obstacles to achieving this include:

1. Perceived costs of adopting environmentally sustainable practices;
2. Lack of knowledge about how to manage environmental performance effectively;
3. A lack of understanding of the value of tourism as a major impediment to growth;
4. Vagueness of the concept of environmental sustainability (e.g. ecotourism and nature based tourism); and
5. Lack of an evidence-based business case.

Strategies

1. Develop and implement an integrated communication program to increase understanding of the significance of tourism's contribution to Victoria's economic and social development and environmental sustainability.
2. Undertake further research to identify the impact of tourism at local, regional and State levels, including the cause and effect relationship of tourism marketing.
3. Raise the industry's profile within Victoria's business and general community. The Victorian Tourism Industry Council is ideally positioned to take a pivotal role in a sustained campaign to raise the profile of the industry and its contribution to Victoria.
4. Tourism Victoria, as a government agency, is well placed to influence a whole of government understanding of tourism, particularly as a priority growth sector on the business agenda. Tourism Victoria should take prime responsibility for implementing the communication program emphasising the value of tourism in the public sector.

5. Strategies in the plan should take into consideration the needs of ethnic and cultural groups.
6. Victorian Tourism Information Service and visitvictoria.com to provide information on tourism opportunities and services for people with disabilities.
7. Due to local government's significant role in tourism development, an on-going program to inform local government about how it can foster and add value to the industry will be maintained.
8. Victoria's tourism industry will develop guidelines for world's best practice principles for environmental sustainability.

Tourism Victoria and the industry will work collaboratively with the Aboriginal tourism sector to realise its potential and integrate the sector with mainstream tourism.

CHAPTER–16

TOURIST ACCOMMODATION

Accommendation is a basic need of tourism activity. Without accommondation it wiil be difficult to develope tourism even in the beautiful places of the world. it's importance could be imagin by imaging what would happened if all accommondation facilities deleted from the tourist places.

Hotel

A hotel is an establishment that provides paid lodging on a short-term basis. The provision of basic accommodation, in times past, consisting only of a room with a bed, a cupboard, a small table and a washstand has largely been replaced by rooms with modern facilities, including en-suite bathrooms and air conditioning or climate control. Additional common features found in hotel rooms are a telephone, an alarm clock, a television, a safe, a mini-bar with snack foods and drinks, and facilities for making tea and coffee. Luxury features include bathrobes and slippers, a pillow menu, twin-sink vanities, and jacuzzi bathtubs. Larger hotels may provide additional guest facilities such as a restaurant, swimming pool, fitness center, business center, childcare, conference facilities and social function services.

Hotel rooms are usually numbered (or named in some smaller hotels and B&Bs) to allow guests to identify their room. Some hotels offer meals as part of a room and board arrangement. In the United Kingdom, a hotel is required by law to serve food and drinks to all guests within certain stated hours. In Japan, capsule hotels provide a minimized amount of room space and shared facilities.

The word *hotel* is derived from the French *hôtel* (coming from *hôte* meaning *host*), which referred to a French version of a townhouse or any other building seeing frequent visitors, rather than a place offering accommodation. In contemporary French usage, *hôtel* now has the same meaning as the English term, and *hôtel particulier* is used for the old meaning. The French spelling, with the circumflex, was also used in English, but is now rare. The circumflex replaces the 's' found in the earlier *hostel* spelling, which over time took on a new, but closely related meaning. Grammatically, hotels usually take the definite article - hence "The Astoria Hotel" or simply "The Astoria."

Types

Hotel operations vary in size, function, and cost. Most hotels and major hospitality companies that operate hotels have set widely accepted industry standards to classify hotel types. General categories include the following;

1. Upscale Luxury
   (a) *Examples include Conrad Hotels, Ritz Carlton, Four Seasons Hotels, and JW Marriott*
2 Full Service
   (a) *Examples include Hilton, Marriott, Doubletree, and Hyatt*
3 Select Service
   (a) *Examples include Courtyard by Marriott and Hilton Garden Inn*
4. Limited Service
   (a) *Examples include Hampton Inn, Fairfield Inn, Days Inn, and La Quinta Inn*

5. Extended Stay
   (a) *Examples include Homewood Suites by Hilton, Residence Inn by Marriott, and Extended Stay Hotels*
6. Timeshare
   (a) *Examples include Marriott Vacation Club, Westgate Resorts, and Disney Vacation Club*
7. Destination Club

Management

The management of a hotel operation is considered a major business operation. Degree programs such as Hospitality management studies and certification programs prepare hotel managers for industry practice.

Historic Hotels

Some hotels have gained their renown through tradition, by hosting significant events or persons, such as Schloss Cecilienhof in Potsdam, Germany, which derives its fame from the Potsdam Conference of the World War II allies Winston Churchill, Harry Truman and Joseph Stalin in 1945. The Taj Mahal Palace & Tower in Mumbai is one of India's most famous and historic hotels because of its association with the Indian independence movement. Some establishments have given name to a particular meal or beverage, as is the case with the Waldorf Astoria in New York City, United States where the Waldorf Salad was first created or the Hotel Sacher in Vienna, Austria, home of the Sachertorte. Others have achieved fame by association with dishes or cocktails created on their premises, such as the Hotel de Paris where the crêpe Suzette was invented or the Raffles Hotel in Singapore, where the Singapore Sling cocktail was devised.

A number of hotels have entered the public consciousness through popular culture, such as the Ritz

Hotel in London, United Kingdom, through its association with Irving Berlin's song, 'Puttin' on the Ritz'. The Algonquin Hotel in New York City is famed as the meeting place of the literary group, the Algonquin Round Table, and Hotel Chelsea, also in New York City, has been the subject of a number of songs and the scene of the stabbing of Nancy Spungen (allegedly by her boyfriend Sid Vicious). The Waldorf Astoria and Statler hotels in New York City are also immortalized in the names of Muppets Statler and Waldorf. The luxurious Grand Hotel Europe in Saint Petersburg, Russia achieved fame with its inclusion in the James Bond film GoldenEye.

Unusual Hotels

Many hotels can be considered destinations in themselves, by dint of unusual features of the lodging or its immediate environment:

Treehouse Hotels

Some hotels are built with living trees as structural elements, for example the Costa Rica Tree House in the Gandoca-Manzanillo Wildlife Refuge, Costa Rica; the Treetops Hotel in Aberdare National Park, Kenya; the Ariau Towers near Manaus, Brazil, on the Rio Negro in the Amazon; and bayram's Tree Houses in Olympos, Turkey.

Bunker Hotels

The Null Stern Hotel in Teufen, Appenzellerland, Switzerland and the Concrete Mushrooms in Albania are former nuclear bunkers transformed into hotels.

Shoe Hotels

Shoe hotels are hotels built into a giant shoe. The idea was inspired by the "Old Woman who lived in a shoe" myth. The largest such hotel is currently in Hokkaido, Japan. The most popular shoe hotels are modelled after a woman's platform dancing shoe.

Cave Hotels

The Cuevas Pedro Antonio de Alarcón (named after the author) in Guadix, Spain, as well as several hotels in Cappadocia, Turkey, are notable for being built into natural cave formations, some with rooms underground. The Desert Cave Hotel in Coober Pedy, South Australia is built into the remains of an opal mine.

Capsule Hotels

Capsule hotels are a type of economical hotel that are found in Japan, where people sleep in stacks of rectangular containers.

Ice and Snow Hotels

The Ice Hotel in Jukkasjärvi, Sweden, and the Hotel de Glace in Duschenay, Canada, melt every spring and are rebuilt each winter; the Mammut Snow Hotel in Finland is located within the walls of the Kemi snow castle; and the Lainio Snow Hotel is part of a snow village near Ylläs, Finland.

Garden Hotels

Garden hotels, famous for their gardens before they became hotels, include Gravetye Manor, the home of garden designer William Robinson, and Cliveden, designed by Charles Barry with a rose garden by Geoffrey Jellicoe.

Underwater Hotels

Some hotels have accommodation underwater, such as Utter Inn in Lake Mälaren, Sweden. Hydropolis, project cancelled 2004 in Dubai, would have had suites on the bottom of the Persian Gulf, and Jules Undersea Lodge in Key Largo, Florida requires scuba diving to access its rooms.

Other Unusual Hotels

1. The Library Hotel in New York City, is unique in that each of its ten floors is assigned one category from the Dewey Decimal System.
2. The Burj al-Arab hotel in Dubai, United Arab Emirates, built on an artificial island, is structured in the shape of a boat's sail.
3. The Jailhotel Löwengraben in Lucerne, Switzerland is a converted prison now used as a hotel.
4. The Luxor, a hotel and casino on the Las Vegas Strip in Paradise, Nevada, United States due to its pyramidal structure.
5. The Liberty Hotel in Boston, used to be the Charles Street Jail.
6. Built in Scotland and completed in 1936, The former ocean liner RMS *Queen Mary* in Long Beach, California, United States uses its first-class staterooms as a hotel, after retiring in 1967 from Transatlantic service.
7. There are several hotels throughout the world built into converted airliners.

Resort Hotels

Some hotels are built specifically to create a captive trade, example at casinos and holiday resorts. Though of course hotels have always been built in popular desinations, the defining characteristic of a resort hotel is that it exists purely to serve another attraction, the two having the same owners.

In Las Vegas there is a tradition of one-upmanship with luxurious and extravagant hotels in a concentrated area known as the Las Vegas Strip. This trend now has extended to other resorts worldwide, but the concentration in Las Vegas is still the world's highest: nineteen of the world's twenty-five largest hotels by room count are on the Strip, with a total of over 67,000 rooms.

In Europe Center Parcs might be considered a chain of resort hotels, since the sites are largely man-made (though set in natural surroundings such as country parks) with captive trade, whereas holiday camps such as Butlins and Pontin's are probably not considered as resort hotels, since they are set at traditional holiday destinations which existed before the camps.

Railway Hotels

Frequently, expanding railway companies built grand hotels at their termini, such as the Midland Hotel, Manchester next to the former Manchester Central Station and in London the ones above St Pancras railway station and Charing Cross railway station also in London is the Chiltern Court Hotel above Baker Street tube station and Canada's grand railway hotels. They are or were mostly, but not exclusively, used by those travelling by rail.

Motels

A motel (motor hotel) is a hotel which is for a short stay, usually for a night, for motorists on long journeys. It has direct access from the room to the vehicle (for example a central parking lot around which the buildings are set), and is built conveniently close to major roads and intersections.

World Record Setting Hotels

Argest

In 2006, Guinness World Records listed the First World Hotel in Genting Highlands, Malaysia as the world's largest hotel with a total of 6,118 rooms. Similarly, the Venetian

Palazzo Complex, in Las Vegas, has the most number of rooms. It has 7,117 rooms followed by MGM Grand Hotel, which contains 6,852 rooms.

Oldest

According to the Guinness Book of World Records, the oldest hotel still in operation is the Hoshi Ryokan, in the Awazu Onsen area of Komatsu, Japan which opened in 718.

Tallest

The Rose Tower in United Arab Emirates is the tallest building used exclusively as a hotel. Originally, the tower was to be 380 m (1,250 ft) high, but design modification reduced it to 333 m (1,093 ft).

Hotel Rooms as an Investment

Some hotels sell individual rooms to investors. Timeshare is an example of this kind of investment. The buyer is allowed to stay in the room without charge or at a reduced rate for a given number of days each year. The investor is paid a share of the takings for the room. Rooms can be sold on a leasehold basis, sometimes on a 999 year lease. Room owners are free to sell at any time.

Living in Hotels

A number of public figures have notably chosen to take up semi-permanent or permanent residence in hotels.

1. Actor Richard Harris lived at the Savoy Hotel while in London. Hotel archivist Susan Scott recounts an anecdote that when he was being taken out of the building on a stretcher shortly before his death he raised his hand and told the diners "it was the food."
2. Inventor Nikola Tesla lived the last 10 years of his life at the New Yorker Hotel until 1943 when he died in the hotel room.

3. Millionaire Howard Hughes lived his last few years in a Las Vegas hotel.
4. Larry Fine (of the Three Stooges) and his family lived in hotels, due to his extravagant spending habits and his wife's dislike for housekeeping. They first lived in the President Hotel in Atlantic City, New Jersey, where his daughter Phyllis was raised, then the Knickerbocker Hotel in Hollywood. Not until the late 1940s did Larry buy a home in the Los Feliz area of Los Angeles, California.
5. General Douglas McArthur lived his last 14 years in the penthouse of the Waldorf Towers, a part of the Waldorf-Astoria Hotel.
6. American actress Elaine Stritch lived in the Savoy Hotel in London for over a decade.
7. Fashion designer Coco Chanel lived in the Hotel Ritz Paris on and off for more than 30 years.
8. Vladimir Nabokov and his wife Vera lived in the Montreux Palace Hotel in Montreux, Switzerland from 1961 until his death in 1977.
9. British entrepreneur Jack Lyons lived in the Hotel Mirador Kempinski in Switzerland for several years until his death in 2008.

House Swapping

House swapping is the practice that refers to the swapping of homes on a temporary or more permanent basis. Although its origins stem from low-cost vacation accommodation and are believed to date back to 1953, there has been an increase in house swapping due to the slow-down in the United States real estate market. Less frequently, it may be used as a method of avoiding violence in war-torn areas.

House swapping is believed to have developed in the 1950s, but rose to prominence in the 1970s as more people got involved and considered it to be a viable vacation option. Some estimates indicate that 15-20% of travelers are participating in some form of house swapping. Summer is traditionally the peak season for house swapping, due to families traveling during summer vacations and house swapping allows families to try out a location for a short period of time while saving money over the traditional vacation costs and allowing them to take vacations that they may otherwise be unable to afford. It's estimated that families can save approximately $5,000 by swapping their homes instead of booking hotels and rental cars, although the perception and listing of the home may not always match reality, and some may be uncomfortable with others using their home. Not all travelers are interested in house swapping solely to save money, but they also see it as a means of meeting locals, seeing relatively un-touristed regions and experiencing local culture. The internet has made the process of finding a swap significantly easier with a number of websites devoted to house swapping.

Eco Hotel

Eco hotel is a term used to describe a hotel or accommodation that has made important environmental improvements to its structure in order to minimize its impact on the environment. The basic definition of a green hotel is an environmentally-responsible lodging that follows the practices of green living. These hotels have to be certified green by an independent third-party or by the state they are located in. Traditionally, these hotels were mostly presented as Eco Lodges because of their location, often in jungles, and their design inspired by the use of traditional building methods applied by skilled local craftsmen in areas, such as Costa Rica and Indonesia. Today, the term has developed to include properties in less "natural" locations that have invested in improving their "green" credentials.

Criteria for Eco-hotel—An eco hotel must usually meet the following criteria :

1. Dependence on the natural environment
2. Ecological sustainability
3. Proven contribution to conservation
4. Provision of environmental training programs
5. Incorporation of cultural considerations
6. Provision of an economic return to the local community

Characteristics of Eco-hotel—Green hotels follow strict green guidelines to ensure that their guests are staying in a safe, non-toxic and energy-efficient accommodation. Here are some basic characteristics of a green hotel:

1. Housekeeping uses non-toxic cleaning agents and laundry detergent
2. 100% organic cotton sheets, towels and mattresses
3. Non-smoking environment
4. Renewable energy sources like solar or wind energy
5. Bulk organic soap and amenities instead of individual packages to reduce waste
6. Guest room and hotel lobby recycling bins
7. Towel and sheet re-use (guests can tell housekeeping to leave these slightly used items to reduce water consumption)
8. Energy-efficient lighting
9. On-site transportation with green vehicles
10. Serve organic and local-grown food
11. Non-disposable dishes
12. Offers a fresh-air exchange system
13. Graywater recycling, which is the reuse of kitchen, bath and laundry water for garden and landscaping
14. Newspaper recycling program

The term has been used on a more regular basis as new websites devoted to the subject become more prominent and hotel owners become more interested in protecting the areas their guests have come to visit.

New properties are being built from sustainable resources–tropical hardwoods, local stone–and designed to better blend in with their environment. In addition, they are also being run on eco-friendly principles, such as serving organic or locally-grown food or using natural cooling as opposed to air conditioning.

Ecolabelling of Hotels in Europe—The EU Ecolabel is an official sign of the environmental quality of services and goods in the European Union (EU) that is both certified by an independent organisation and valid throughout the many member States of the European Union.

Any tourism accommodation operator in the EU - from a large hotel chain to a small farmhouse has been able to apply for the European Eco-label since 2003. The operators must meet strict minimum standards with regard to environmental performance and health standards. These should include the use of renewable energy sources, an overall reduction in energy and water consumption, measures to reduce waste, environmental policy setting and the provision of non-smoking areas.

The first eco-labelled hotel in the European Union was the Sunwing Resort Kallithea, located in Rhodes, Greece in 2003 and the first eco-labelled hotel on the Iberian Peninsula (Spain and Portugal) was the Hotel Jardim Atlântico on the Portuguese island of Madeira.

Homestay

Homestay is a form of tourism and/or study abroad program that allows the visitor to rent a room from a local family to better learn the local lifestyle as well as improve their language ability. While homestays can occur in any destination worldwide, some countries do more to encourage homestay than others as a means of developing their tourism industry. Hosting a homestay participant also allows the local family to earn some additional, needed income. Having low profitability, as it is, homestay can not be regarded as strictly commercial activity, but more of cross cultural exchange.Students generally arrange a homestay with their school or educational institution, but can also informally arrange to stay with a family through social connections, and through a variety of private agencies. There are a number of online homestay agencies that connect students with hosts all over the world (usually for a nominal fee).

Homestay scenarios can range from a completely immersive family experience, to a very basic room rental.

In the immersive family experience a homestay student lives, eats, and shares the majoritiy of their time in the host country with the hosts and their family. Family events such as dining out, amusement parks, camping, travel, etc. usually involve the host student who may or may not be expected to pay a portion for the participation (tickets, parking, gas, travel expenses, et al.) The student is invited to participate in Holiday festivities (Thanksgiving, Christmas, etc.) and family events (weddings, birthdays, etc.)

At the other end of the spectrum, students may simply be renting a room within a private home with minimal supervision from a host or family. Additionally, there are a working homestay agreements where a student is expected to perform duties such as yard work, farm work, babysitting, maid services - usually in exchange for accommodation fees or as part of.

Typically, hosting a homestay student is a rich and rewarding experience that allows the sharing of cultures, information, and experience. However, studying abroad is often the first time the homestay student is away from the parents and home country. This may result in adjustment issues for the student. The host must be able to deal with separation issues, anxiety, and the like.

Scams on the internet are becoming fairly commonplace - when engaging in financial transactions that may require international payments, cheques, and money orders being sent there is always the possibility of making oneself vulnerable to scams and fraud. The host family is best to educate themselves on the issues, and protect themselves adequately through the use of a good contract.

A recent and common example of a scamperpetrated on host families plays as follows;

1. Parents of a student email the host family to request a room - usually claiming to be from Europe/Asia.
2. The host replies with availability and costs etc.
3. The parent agrees to the fees, and offers to pay the fees up front.
4. Usually some sort of family crisis arises, and the transaction must be handled with urgency.
5. The parent sends payment with an overage, and aks the host to refund the excess payment.
6. The host family refunds the payment.
7. The initial payment (cheque, money order, etc.) bounces or is fraudulent.
8. The host family has lost the money it has sent as a refund.

This scam can happen in any situation any time payment is required in the form of cheque/money order/cashiers cheque, etc. In-depth discussion on frauds of this type is beyond the scope of this article, but the host family is encouraged to exercise caution when dealing with overseas payments and transactions.

Vacation Rental

Vacation rental is a term in the US travel industry meaning renting out a furnished apartment or house on a temporary basis to tourists as an alternative to a hotel. Other parts of the world refer to holiday homes or holiday apartments. Vacation rentals have long been a popular travel option in Europe (especially in the UK) as well as in Canada and are becoming increasingly popular across the world. They are often referred to as self-catering rentals or villa rentals. In some cities, like Barcelona, local authorities determined that vacation rentals were becoming a threat to the hotel industry and passed some legislation placing regulations and limits on the industry, while in others, such as England, Ireland, France and Spain, the government promotes and certifies holiday rentals, even offering its own program of holiday/vacation rentals.

A vacation rental is a fully furnished property, such as a holiday cottage, condominium, townhome or single-family-style home, often referred to as villa rentals in Europe. The client/traveler arranges to rent the vacation rental property for a designated period of time, many rent on nightly basis similar to hotel rooms, although the more prevalent vacation rental industry practice is typically weekly rentals. A true vacation rental is not for sale to the guest; rather, the owner of the vacation rental merely allows the guest to rent the property for a predetermined length of time.

Gîtc

A gîte (masculine gender, French pronunciation:) is a French holiday home that is available for rent. Gîtes are usually fully furnished and equipped for self-catering. Many owners choose to handle their own rentals, and you can find these by searching online on the multitude of listing sites or by checking with the local tourist information office.

Technically speaking, to be called a gîte, the owner must live close by in order to provide help, assistance, and a warm welcome to guests. Gîtes are generally old farmworkers' cottages or converted outbuildings and barns within proximity of the owners' principal residence. This type of holiday accommodation is sometimes regarded as 'basic' in terms of facilities; however, most gîtes are generally very well kept, and a growing number will have excellent facilities such as fully fitted kitchens, en-suite bathrooms, TV, DVD and access to a swimming pool or other sporting activities. The term gîte nowadays encompasses most forms of holiday cottage and even holiday flats or apartments. Many gites will also accept pets.

The term *gîte* originally meant quite simply a form of shelter. Gîtes today vary from being luxury holiday homes to very basic apartments. Some gîtes don t provide linen as standard, so many gîte holiday makers take their linen with them. However, many gîte owners do include linen at least as an option. Gîtes are encouraged by the local tourist board and planning authorities as they attract investment and tourism. All gîte owners are required to ensure that their gîtes are safe and comply with the necessary rules, regulations and insurance requirements.

Intervac International

Intervac International is a worldwide organisation that facilitates exchanges of homes ("home exchange" or "house swapping") for vacations. Proponents of this form of travel call it culturally-enriching, comfortable and economic - while promoting international contacts and understanding. Intervac was founded in 1953. It is the longest operating home exchange service. Intervac currently has on average 10,000 members based in 50 countries worldwide.

Lodging

Lodging (or a holiday accommodation) is a type of residential accommodation. People who travel and stay away from home for more than a day need lodging for sleep, rest, safety, shelter from cold temperatures or rain, storage of luggage and access to common household functions.

Lodgings may be *self catering* in which case no food is laid on but cooking facilities are available. Lodging is done in a hotel, hostel or hostal, a private home (commercial, i.e. a bed and breakfast, a guest house, a vacation rental, or non-commercially, with members of hospitality services or in the home of friends), in a tent, caravan/camper (often on a campsite). In addition there are make-shift solutions.

Sleeping is typically done lying in a bed, or more generally on a soft surface, such as an air mattress, a couch, etc. Some trains have sleeping cars. Sometimes people sleep sitting, because lying is not possible, such as in a train (if not in a sleeping car), a bus, a seat in a waiting room or a bench on the street or in a park. Inclinable seats allow something between sitting and lying. Whether lying on a row of seats is possible and comfortable depends on the presence of arm rests, and whether they can be moved up. In some public places, lying would be possible, but is not permitted.

CHAPTER–17

INTERNATIONAL ORGANIZATION

National Tourist Administration (NTAs)

The rapid spread of education led to the desire to find out how people live in other countries. Governments helped in the promotion of tourism by setting up National Tourist Organisations, initially to promote inbound tourism to their country. Some countries actively promoted the concept of overseas travel among their own nationals. Take the case of Japan—this small country of one hundred and twenty million people sends fifteen million tourists to foreign lands every year— more than one out of ten Japanese! The Japanese Government considers it a way of balancing their huge trade surplus with other countries. The Japanese who come to India, for instance, spend money in India. And, the Indian Government which has an unfavourable balance of trade with Japan, can balance the trade gap to some extent.

Over fifty-five million trips to foreign countries are taken by the US citizens every year—and the total US population is a little more than two hundred and eighty million! Domestic tourism, too is an essential part of the lifestyles of Americans, Europeans and the Japanese. Two or three domestic holidays in one year are not uncommon.

Why People Travel

Anybody who travels has a motive of his or her own. On the basis of these motives or purposes, we can divide tourism into distinct categories.

Recreational Travel

The first and foremost is recreational travel. The purpose in this case is recreation—holiday or leisure. People want to get away from the humdrum of everyday life and move to beaches, mountains and the scenic countryside. It has been estimated that seventy-five per cent of international travel in the world and fifty per cent of domestic travel is recreational. According to an Indian Government Survey, done in 1999, seventy-five per cent of foreign visitors come to India for recreation or holiday and the remaining twenty-five per cent come for business, official visits and other purposes.

Adventure and Sports Tourism

The trips undertaken by people for playing golf, tennis, skiing, trekking, mountaineering, etc., fall within this category. Adventure tourism is becoming a popular form of tourism in India. The country offers many opportunities for an adventure holiday and it is becoming more popular.

Cultural Tourism

The third category is cultural tourism. When people are motivated to travel in order to see the cultural heritage of their own country or those of foreign countries, i.e., visit ancient

historical monuments, places of religious interest, museums, art galleries, etc., it is termed as cultural tourism. Visits to Varanasi, Haridwar or Rameshwaram are part of cultural tourism.

Health Tourism

The fourth category is that of people who take trips to have medical treatment elsewhere, or to visit places where there are curative possibilities such as hot springs, spas or yoga institutes. This is called health tourism. People travelling to Kerala for ayurvedic treatment or to the USA for major surgeries, fall in this category.

Conference and Convention Tourism

In recent years, two new, but very important categories of tourism have emerged—convention and conference tourism. A large number of people are now travelling within their own country, or abroad to attend conventions or conferences, attending meetings relating to their businesses. The purpose is to gain knowledge through other people's experiences. This is a fast-growing area of travel. In many countries like the USA and Japan, expenditure incurred by company executives on attending business-related conferences overseas, is tax-deductible. If a doctor from the USA or Japan comes to India to attend a medical conference, his expenditure on his Indian trip will be tax-deductible. The Government of India does not extend similar concessions to its professionals as yet.

Incentive Travel

The concept of incentive travel was developed to motivate workers to do a better job. The manufacturing companies or business corporations offer their good workers, sales executives, retailers or wholesalers with rewards of free holidays within the country or overseas which include transportation, hotels, meals and entertainment. People seem to prefer free holidays as a reward, as compared to material gifts like a TV set, refrigerator or a washing machine. In affluent countries, workers often do not need these items as incentives as they have already bought them from their own savings. So, the idea of offering free holidays as an incentive was discovered and has since caught on. Often, the incentive includes free travel, both for husband and wife. Every year, millions of people are travelling as part of incentive travel from their companies in different parts of the world. In countries like the USA, there are travel companies specialising in organising incentive travel only for business corporations. Incentive travel for workers and executives has started in India too—though the scale is as yet modest. Some companies promote foreign tours to neighbouring countries.

Organisation of Tourism

Having determined what makes people travel, we can look at the organisation of tourism in the world. We have discussed in an earlier chapter, the role of travel agents who act as coordinators of different segments of travel.

Travel has become a massive business enterprise. In some countries it has assumed the shape of mass tourism. Imagine, Spain with a population of ten million—had forty-eight million foreign visitors in 2000) had Even in Asia, Singapore has a population of 2.4 million and foreign visitors were seven million in 2000.

Role of Government

Governments, therefore, have to play a key role in the planning, development, regulation and marketing of tourism. Tourism helps every government because it provides employment to the citizens and earns foreign currency for the country. Therefore, practically every government in the world, irrespective of its size, has a NTA. It may be called a Department of Tourism as in the case of India, a Tourist Promotion Board as in the case of Singapore, a Tourism Authority as in the UK and Thailand or a Tourism Ministry as in the Philippines. The NTAs are involved in planning, development, promotion and administration of tourism. While planning a beach or mountain resort, an NTA tries to make sure that there is no overcrowding, pollution and destruction of historic or archaeological landmarks as a result of the new area development for tourism. To promote tourism, an NTA opens tourist offices overseas to attract foreign tourists to their shores. They also have tourist information offices within their own countries, to provide information to foreign visitors on arrival and also to domestic travellers who wish to travel within their own country.

In India, the Central Department of Tourism has eleven tourist offices in foreign countries and twenty-one within India. In large countries like India, there are several Government tourist organisations. For instance, almost all the twenty-eight State Governments of India and seven Union Territories have their Departments of Tourism and majority of them have Government-owned State Tourism Development Corporations. They operate at State levels. Although most States have their Departments of Tourism and Tourism Development Corporations, the level of tourism development has been uneven. Tourism is a State subject and the Centre cannot enforce its decisions unilaterally on all the States. It was in this context that the National Committee on Tourism (NCT), suggested in 1988 that tourism should be brought on the concurrent list of the Constitution of India, as quoted at the beginning of this chapter. The advantage would be that the Central Government could initiate a legislation in the tourism field for All-India application. Initially State Governments were not interested in tourism development. The Centre had to subsidise the State Governments to open such departments for promotion of tourism. Now most of them are reasonably active and are no longer subsidised by the Centre. The Centre, however, assists them financially to strengthen or streamline their infrastructure where needed.

At the All-India level, there is the public sector—India Tourism Development Corporation (ITDC), with a network of hotels all over India, transport units in various states, a chain of duty-free shops at the international airports and undertaking other tourism-related jobs. Several States have followed the ITDC pattern at their level. Now, a decision has been taken at the Centre that the Government should leave the tourism business to private sector. ITDC is, therefore, in the process of privatisation and the State Governments too are thinking on similar lines. In fact, these Corporations with so much public investments have become a burden on public exchequer, as they are no longer profitable. The Government has to put in money to run them.

World Tourism Organisation

In the organisational chart of tourism, World Tourism Organisation (WTO) is the apex body—representing at world level, the tourism interests of NTAs and working as an affiliate of the United Nations Organisation (UNO). Started as the International Union of Official Travel Organisation (IUOTO) in the first half of the twentieth century, it became an inter-governmental organisation in 1975 and named World Tourism Organisation WTO, for short. Presently, it has a membership of one hundred and thirty-seven countries and territories. Besides, there are some three hundred and fifty affiliate members like airlines, travel agencies, etc.

WTO provides many services to its members—principal one being the compilation of travel statistics and the publication of books and reports, to help member Governments to plan and develop their tourism. It works closely with several other international organisation with the objectives of helping develop tourism in the world. It offers expert help to developing countries to plan, develop and reorganise their tourism. It strives to improve the quality of tourism education. Presently, its focus is to create environment for sustainable tourism.

India is one of its founding members and is often elected to its Executive Council. Its Chief Executive is called Secretary General. WTO aims to create favourable conditions for free movement of travel in the world. For this purpose, it favours the passport-free travel in the world. To some extent, it has been achieved in all the European countries (EU), where the citizens can travel without visa and passport. Besides, they have introduced a common currency called Euro making travel hassle-free. At present, if a visitor gets visa for one of the eleven European countries, it is valid for all the eleven member countries. WTO is based in Madrid, Spain.

Pacific Asia Travel Association (PATA)

Among other world bodies which sustain and promote international tourism, Pacific Asia Travel Association (PATA) is notable. Although its active members are from the Pacific region, extending from Canada to the Indian sub-continent, (hundred governments, sixty-six airlines and cruise lines. Its presence, etc., worldwide is felt through its more than eighty chapters (seventeen thousand members). It is primarily a marketing organisation, promoting tourism to the Pacific region and assisting member countries in various ways.

Originally established in Hawaii in 1951, it was later headquartered in San Francisco for four decades and is now based in Bangkok, with divisional offices in USA, Australia, Singapore and Europe. It membership exceeds 2000 and consists of governments, airlines, steamship companies, cruise lines, travel agencies, media, etc.

PATA is headed by a Chief Executive and managed by a large Board of Directors, representing many countries. Its annual conventions are a great draw, attracting some one thousand five hundred industry leaders from all over the world. The 2002 Convention was held in New Delhi.

PATA organisation is actively involved in developing ethos for sustainable tourism.

PATA programmes are designed to meet the needs of members, allowing each to remain competitive in the world market place. PATA offers to its members research and marketing services, product development and a variety of educational seminars and workshops.

Besides the above, there are world organisations representing hotels, travel agencies, airlines, transport, etc. We will read about them under different chapters.

In the organisation of tourism, transport is an inseparable element. Tourism transport consists of aeroplanes, motor vehicles, railways, cruise lines, etc. Of course, governments are closely involved in the operation and regulation of the transport system.

Another essential element of tourism is accommodation—hotels, motels, inns, tourist bungalows or lodges, youth hostels, etc., where tourists can stay. (We have a separate chapter on this subject).

Finally, the most important elements are the tourist attractions of a country—scenic beauty, historical monuments, rivers, lakes, parks, mountains, beaches, forests, wildlife, flora and fauna, climate, food and shopping. Tourists come to see and enjoy what a country can offer. Together, all the elements mentioned above, comprise the tourism assets or resources of a country. When these are packaged, the experts call it the 'tourism product' of a country. After all, this is the product a visitor wants to buy. Like manufactured products, the tourism product too has a lot of variety. You can package it in many interesting ways as preferred or demanded by the customers. It may be a holiday on the beaches, a peep into a country's past, a mountain vacation, wildlife viewing or a shopping tour. The visitors have several options and combinations of options at different price ranges.

There is, however, one difference. Tourism is a product which has to be bought unseen. Like manufactured products, you cannot bring them to the customer to see and feel. The customer has to go to it to experience and to feel it! The new technology however, can present to you, on a computor, 'virtual reality' of the tourism product.

India's National Tourist Administration (NTA)

As mentioned earlier, every country sets up its National Tourist Administration (NTA) according to its own requirements. All countries or States of the world, have a NTA, supported and sponsored by the Government of the country. In the western world, most NTAs are sponsored and financed by the Government. In a few countries, private sector also supports it financially and is involved, to some extent, in the management of NTAs. This is not so in India.

The Department of Tourism which manages tourism at the Government level, is wholly dependent on the Government for financial support. No attempt has been made to involve the private sector financially in a supporting role. The private sector is not involved even in an advisory role, though it is sometimes consulted at the discretion of the Goverment.

The argument in favour of private sector participation is that since the private sector is the major beneficiary of tourism promotion undertaken by a Government, it is logical that they share part of the expenditure on tourism promotion and management. The Government of India, in its wisdom, decided not to involve the private sector. Or, when the Government of India mooted the idea of promoting tourism, the private sector was not strong enough to contribute any money. A successful example of the Government and the private sector being actively involved in the NTO affairs is Switzerland, where the private sector contributes almost forty per cent of the expenditure. USA does not have a

NTA—it was disbanded in 1995 for economic reasons. Federal Government felt that the private sector should solely promote tourism as they were the primary beneficiaries. And, US tourism has not since looked back.

There were valid reasons for not involving the private sector. When the Department of Tourism was set up in 1958, the travel industry in India was so small and so shy that the Government did not think that the industry could contribute substantially. So, the idea of charging a fee from the industry did not appeal to the decision-makers.

In fact, the private sector in hoteliering and transport was so reluctant that the Government of India had to set up a company in the public sector to build and operate hotels at tourist centres, where the private sector was not willing to invest. Similarly, at major tourist centres like Khajuraho, Varanasi or Jaipur, there was no adequate tourist transport facilities. The public sector company, ITDC with its headquarters in New Delhi, had to step in to operate public sector transport units to provide good transport fleet.

India, therefore, is a unique case history in tourism development.

During the early years of independence, major business houses, except the house of Tatas, did not consider the operation of hotels and restaurants as an honourable business. There were only a few modern hotels in the country and those too run by foreigners. The Government's intervention became necessary to develop the basic infrastructure at major tourist centres to attract foreign tourists. This led to the Government building and operating hotels and transport units, through its public sector organisation like the ITDC all over India. State Tourism Corporations have followed the same pattern and built budget accommodation and have also operated tourist transport fleets in their respective States.

The tourism scene has changed drastically during the last thirty years and the private sector is now very active in tourism development. Indian hotels in the private sector compare favourably with the best in the world and some of the leading Indian hotel chains are operating hotels in developed countries under their brand name. The Government of India has recognised this fact and decided not to invest any more in the construction of new five-star hotels, leaving the tourism industry totally open to the private sector in India. In fact, there are moves to sell hotels owned by ITDC and Hotel Corporation of India. A few properties were sold in 2002.

India's NTA would, therefore, consist of a Department of Tourism which is a Department of the Ministry of Tourism and also the India Tourism Development Corporation which is a public sector company and implements Government's policy decisions in tourism field. The WTO has a new name for NTOs— the National Tourism Administration—NTAs. They prefer to call it NTA because an Administration has wider ramifications than the Organisation.

The private sector is encouraged by the Department of Tourism to operate tourism facilities under the overall policy guidelines of the Government. In fact, there is an excellent cooperation and understanding between the Department of Tourism and the private sector tour operators, travel agents, transporters and hoteliers in the area of tourism development. Historically, tourism development in India has suffered due to a lack of clear thinking on the part of political decision-makers in the country. Bureaucratic hurdles made it worse.

India became aware of the importance of tourism promotion as early as in 1946. Sir John Sargent, Educational Adviser to the Government of India, headed a committee to survey the potential of tourism in India and recommended that developing tourist traffic, both internal and external, will be beneficial for India. The recommendation led to the establishment of a Tourist Traffic branch in the Ministry of Transport and Communication, with a network of tourist offices in India and abroad. The branch later transformed itself into a department headed by a director general in 1958. The first overseas tourist office was set up in New York as early as in 1952, followed by similar offices in London, Paris, Frankfurt, Colombo, Melbourne and San Francisco. In retrospect, tourist offices overseas were opened too soon at too many foreign cities without providing them adequate budgetary support and without analysing the availability of adequate infrastructure at home, particularly accommodation suitable for foreigners. Besides, travellers from distant countries like USA, Canada, had a poor image of India as a holiday destination.

CHAPTER–18

THE FINANCES

Finance is the science of funds management. The general areas of finance are *business finance, personal finance,* and *public finance.* Finance includes saving money and often includes lending money. The field of finance deals with the concepts of time, money, risk and how they are interrelated. It also deals with how money is spent and budgeted.

One facet of finance is through individuals and business organizations, which deposit money in a bank. The bank then lends the money out to other individuals or corporations for consumption or investment and charges interest on the loans.

Loans have become increasingly packaged for resale, meaning that an investor buys the loan (debt) from a bank or directly from a corporation. Bonds are debt instruments sold to investors for organizations such as companies, governments or charities. The investor can then hold the debt and collect the interest or sell the debt on a secondary market. Banks are the main facilitators of funding through the provision of credit, although private equity, mutual funds, hedge funds, and other organizations have become important as they invest in various forms of debt. Financial assets, known as investments, are financially managed with careful attention to financial risk management to control financial risk. Financial instruments allow many forms of securitized assets to be traded on securities exchanges such as stock exchanges, including debt such as bonds as well as equity in publicly traded corporations.

Central banks, such as the Federal Reserve System banks in the United States and Bank of England in the United Kingdom, are strong players in public finance, acting as lenders of last resort as well as strong influences on monetary and credit conditions in the economy.

Tourism Industry Growth

The Ministry of Tourism in any country seeks ways to promote and develop tourism in the country. **Tourism Industry Growth**in any country is prone to the changing economic conditions. In the event when a country is passing through a low phase or an individual's job is at stake, not many people choose to travel. This poses a limitation in the spending power of the individuals. People under these circumstances tend to settle for low budget restaurants, hotels or opt for amusement parks and nearby places.

Tourism and Economy

Occasionally, Tourism Industry is subjected to several snags. These hindrances causes the economy of a country to become slow, resulting in the GDP or gross domestic productivity being slow and consequently employment opportunities get affected.

Improving Tourism Industry Growth

The Ministry of Tourism adopts many policies to counteract hurdles and obstacles which come in the way of the development of Tourism in a country. Policies adopted by Ministry of Tourism are aimed at enhancing services and tourism tools to attract as many tourists as possible. This also includes working on Eco tourism projects. Every possible effort is made to set standards as per norms of the World tourism Industry.

Tourism Improvements Programs

Tourism improvement programs aim at:

1. Making the marketing tools and promotional tools strong
2. Employ trained personnel
3. Make the programs act as catalyst in investments by private bodies.
4. Propounding projects and programs at the national level.
5. Carry out research work for the betterment of the Tourism industry.
6. Infrastructure is developed.

Tourism Related Industries

There are many industries which are closely associated with other industries offering services to the common people. These industries can be summed up as below:

1. Hotels, Lodging services
2. F&B or food and beverage industry
3. Industry dealing with real estate, finance, leasing and insurance.
4. Retail market
5. Warehousing and transport industry.

Economic Significance

Tourism has major economic significance for a country. The receipts from international tourism can provide a valuable source of earnings for many countries both developed as well as developing. Visitor-spending generates income for both public and private sector besides affecting wages and employment opportunities. Although tourism is sensitive to the level of economic activity in the tourist-generating countries, it provides more fixed earnings than primary products. The income from tourism has tended to increase at a higher rate than merchandise export in a number of countries specially in countries having a low industrial base. There is now an almost assured channel for financial flows from the developed countries to the developing countries raising the latter's export earnings and rate of economic growth. Tourism therefore provides a most important source of income for a number of countries both developed and developing. According to World Tourism Organisation (WTO), among the world's top 40 tourism earners about 18 were developing countries including India, in the year 1995. Regarding the number of visitor arrivals, in some countries there were more visitor arrivals than the population. France with a population of 57 million received 74.5 million visitors in the year 2000. Similarly Spain with a population of 37 million received 48.5 million visitors during the same year. Several island countries in such areas as Caribbean depend very heavily on tourist income resulting from visitor arrivals, which often the represents the major part of the gross domestic product (G.D.P.). Even developed countries like Canada which derived over 13 per cent of its gross domestic product from international visitors in the year 1999 rely heavily on income from tourism. Tourism thus forms a very important source of income, especially foreign exchange, for several countries. Although the quantum contributed in foreign currency per visitor varies from one destination to another, the importance of receipts from tourism in the balance of payment accounts and of tourist activities in the national revenue, has become considerable for a number of countries.

The major economic benefit in promoting the tourism industry has therefore, tended to be the earning of foreign exchange. Income from foreign tourism in the form of foreign-exchange earnings adds to the national income and, as an invisible export, may offset a loss on the visible trading account and be of critical importance in the overall financial reckoning. This is more true in the case of developing countries particularly the small countries, mainly dependent upon primary products such as a few basic cash crops where tourism often offers a more reliable form of income. In the case of some European countries, notably Spain, Portugal, Austria, France and Greece, the invisible earnings from tourism are of a major significance and have a very strong positive effect on the balance of payments. Tourism is thus a very useful means of earning the much-needed foreign currency. It is almost without a rival as an earning source for many developed as well as developing countries. These earnings assume a great significance in the balance of payment calculations.

The balance of payments shows the relationship between a country's total payments to all other countries and its total receipts from them. In other words, it may be defined as a statement of income and expenditure on international account. Payments and receipts on international account are of three kinds (i) the visible balance of trade relating to the import and export of goods (ii) invisible items (relating to the services such as shipping and insurance); (iii) capital transfers. The receipts from foreign tourism form an 'invisible export', similar to other invisibles which come from transportation and shipping, banking and insurance, income on investments, etc. Because most countries at times have serious problems with their international payments, much attention comes to be focussed on tourism because of its potentially important contribution to, and also effect upon, the balance of payments.

The receipts from international tourism, however, are not always net. Sometimes expenditures are involved which must be set against them. Net foreign exchange receipts from tourism are reduced principally by the import cost of goods and services used by visitors, foreign exchange costs of capital investment in tourist amenities and promotion and publicity expenditure abroad. Peters has said: "Certain imports associated with tourist expenditures must be deduced...the importation of material and equipment for constructing hotels and other amenities, and necessary supplies to run them; foreign currency costs of imports for consumption by international tourists; remittances of interests and profits on overseas investment in tourism enterprises, mainly hotel construction; foreign currency costs of conducting a tourism development programme, including marketing expenditure overseas."

Reliance on imports to meet the tourist's needs does not, however, deny developing countries the opportunity of earning foreign exchange in supplying such goods and services. Imports are, to a large extent, as essential to the operation of the tourist sector as to that of other sectors. The important question is whether the value added domestically on an export item or service is maximised. Maximisation of import substitution without due regard to the effect on overall tourism receipts (i.e., demand) may be counter-productive. Secondly, differences in the pattern and level of reliance on imported goods and services, capital equipment and manpower are very wide, depending upon the level of development of a country. In some cases, this reliance is simply due to a lack of resources that will be transformed into items to be sold to the industry. In others, the industry has not yet drawn on such supply potential, for which it may be an important stimulus. There is a general need for careful programmes of positive import substitution.

Tourism Multiplier

It is evident from the above paragraphs that earnings from tourism occupy an important place in the national income of a country. Without taking into account receipts from domestic tourism, international tourism receipts alone contribute a great deal. The flow of money generated by tourist spending multiplies as it passes through various sections of the economy. In addition to an important source of income, tourism provides a number of other economic benefits, which vary in importance from one country to another, depending upon the nature and scale of tourism. The benefits from infrastructure investments, justified primarily for tourism such as airports, roads, water supply and other public utilities, may be widely shared by the other sectors of the economy. Tourist facilities such as hotels, restaurants, museums, clubs, sports complexes, public transport, national parks are used also by domestic tourists and visitors, businessmen and residents, yet a significant portion of the costs may be borne by international tourists. Tourists also contribute to tax revenue both directly through sales tax and indirectly through property, profits and income taxes. Tourism provides employment, brings infrastructural improvements and may help regional development. Each of these economic aspects can be dealt with separately, but they are all closely related and are considered together. Let us first look at the income aspect of tourism.

Tourism as a source of income is not easy to measure, at least with any degree of accuracy. This is because of the multiplier effect. The flow of money generated by tourist spending multiplies as it passes through various sections of the economy through the operation of the multiplier effect. The multiplier is an income concept.

The Concept

The 'multiplier' measures the impact of extra expenditure introduced into an economy by a person. It is, therefore, concerned with the marginal rather than average changes. In the case of tourism, this extra expenditure in a particular area can take various forms, including the following:

1. Spending on goods and services by tourists visiting the areas;
2. Investment of external sources in tourism infrastructure or services.

3. Government (foreign or domestic) spending (e.g., domestic government spending on infrastructure in a region or foreign government aid); and
4. Exports of goods stimulated by tourism;

The expenditure can be analysed as follows:

(i) Direct Expenditure: In the case of tourism, this expenditure is made by tourists on goods and services in hotels, other forms of supplementary accommodation units, restaurants, other tourist facilities like buses, taxis coaches, railways, domestic airlines, and for tourism-generated exports, or by tourism related investment in the area.

(ii) Indirect Expenditure: This covers successive rounds of inter-business transaction which result from the direct expenditure, such as purchase of goods by hoteliers from local suppliers and purchases by local suppliers from wholesalers.

(iii) Induced Expenditure: This is the increased consumer spending resulting from the additional personal income generated by the direct expenditure, e.g., hotel workers using their wages for the purchase of goods and services. Indirect and induced expenditure together are called secondary expenditure.

There are several different concepts of the multiplier. The four types of multipliers are intrinsically linked and those in common use are:

(i) Sales (Transaction) Multiplier : This measures the extra business turnover created (direct and secondary) by an extra unit of tourist expenditure,

(ii) Output Multiplier: This is similar to the sales multiplier but it also takes into account inventory changes, such as the increase in stock levels by hotels, restaurants and shops because of increased trading activity.

(iii) Income Multiplier: This measures the income generated by an extra unit of tourist expenditure. The

problem arises over the definition of income. Many researchers define income as disposable income accruing to households within the area, which is available to them to spend. However, although salaries paid to overseas residents are often excluded, a proportion of these salaries may be spent in the local area and should therefore be included.

Income Multipliers can be expressed in two ways: the *ratio method* which expresses the direct and indirect incomes (or the direct and secondary incomes) generated per unit of direct income; or the *normal method,* which expresses total income (direct and secondary) generated in the study area per unit increase in final demand created within a particular sector.

Ratio multipliers indicate the internal linkages which exist between various sectors of the economy, but do not relate income generated to extra sales. Hence, on their own, ratio multipliers are valueless as a planning tool.

(iv) Employment Multiplier: This can be expressed in one of the two ways: as a ratio of the combination of direct and secondary employment generated per additional unit of tourist expenditure to direct employment created by tourism per unit of tourist expenditure. Multipliers can be further categorised by the geographical area which is covered by the research, such as local community, a region within a country or a country as a whole.

Models

Multiplier evaluation necessitates the use of models. The degree of sophistication of these models varies. However, there are three elemental forms:

(i) Base Model: This is very simplistic and rarely used in practical research. It assumes that one can divide the economy under research into export activities and local (non-export) activities, and that a stable relationship exists between the export and local sectors, with these sectors linked by linear relationships. It further assumes that unemployed resources are available within the economy, and that the scale of the export activities is the sole determinant of the level of income and employment within the area.

(ii) Keynesian Model: This is based on identifying streams of income and employment which are generated in "rounds", which diminish in geometric progression because of leakages at each round.

(iii) Input-output Model: The input-output concept analyses the economy into its sectors and expresses a relationship of these sectors in matrix form, based on the results of research into the effects of tourist expenditure.

Most multipliers in common use incorporate the general principle of the Keynesian model. These have been developed into modified forms of input-output analysis with separate formulae being utilised for each principal business activity-one for businesses which are not primarily dependent upon tourism expenditure and will continue to exist without it, and the second for businesses which are dependent on tourism for their existence.

Fundamental to multiplier research is the concept of "leakages" from the economy. It is such leakages which result in rounds of income and employment, identified in Keynesian models, diminishing. The exact nature of these leakages will depend on the characteristics of the particular study. Some examples of leakages are as follows:

1. Payment for goods and services produced outside, and imported into, the study area;
2. Remittance of incomes outside the study area, for example, by foreign workers;
3. Indirect and direct taxation where the tax proceeds are not re-spent in the study area;
4. Savings out of income received by workers in the study area (i.e., where there is a low propensity to consume).

The multiplier theory emerges from the works of Kahn and Keynes. In simple terms it can be systematically explained as follows:

"From an initial impulse, such as investment or expenditure, there springs one or more primary effects such as income, savings, etc. These primary effects in their turn, and in the course of a second period, produce secondary effects of the same type as the first. The process is repeated several times in a given passage of time. The multiplier makes it possible to calculate the sum of the various primary, secondary and tertiary, effects of the same type and hence the relation between the total of the effects of the same nature and the primary effect. This relation is represented by the multiplier, which is then applied to the primary effect in order to arrive at the total effect".

The multiplier mechanism has also been applied to tourism and, in particular, to tourist expenditure. The nature of the tourism multiplier and its effect may be described as follows: "The money paid by a tourist in, say, paying his hotel bill will be used by the hotel management to provide for the costs which it had incurred in meeting the demands of the visitor, e.g., such goods and services as food, drink, furnishing, laundering, electricity, and entertainment. The recipients, in turn, use the money they have thus received to meet their financial commitments and so on. In other words, tourist expenditure not only supports the tourist industry directly but helps indirectly to support many other industries which supply goods and services to the tourist industry. In this way money spent by tourists may be said to be used several times and to spread into various sectors of the economy. In sum, the money paid by the tourist, after a long series of transfers over a given period of time, passes through all sectors of the national economy, stimulating each in turn throughout the process".

Every time the money changes hands it provides 'new' income and the continuing series of conversions of the money spent by the tourists form what the economists term the multiplier effect. The more often the conversion occurs, the greater its beneficial effect on the economy of the recipient country. However, this transfer of money is not absolute as there are 'leakages' which occur. Such leakages may occur as a result of, importing foreign goods, paying interest on foreign investments, etc. Any leakages of these kinds will reduce the stream of expenditure which, in consequence, will limit and reduce the multiplier effect. Income generated by foreign tourist expenditure in countries possessing more advanced economies, which generally are more self-sufficient and less in need of foreign imports, will tend to have higher multipliers than countries which are less self-sufficient and need to support their tourist industries by substantial imports. If the developing countries are to gain maximum economic benefits from tourism, they should control very strictly those imported items for tourist consumption and to keep foreign investment expenditure to a reasonable level.

The benefits otherwise accruing from tourism will reduce or even be cancelled by the leakages.

The most important leakage would appear to arise from expenditures on importation of agricultural products like food and drink. In a primary macro-economic approach to the prospects opened up by tourism establishment in a developing country, it is regarded as advantageous that a good portion of tourist consumption should consist of food products. It is estimated that the major part of these products can be found in those countries, whose economic structure is largely agricultural in character. In this sense tourist consumption, derived from international flow, can offer an assured outlet to a production which is already active within the country, without raising problems connected with export of such products in the international markets. Home-grown products could thus be substituted for imported foodstuffs and a significant saving effected.

Such savings would help to increase the tourism multiplier, which in turn would help the host country to derive maximum economic benefits from its tourist industry. This aspect of the question is all the more important in that the multiplier effect maintains its efficacy as long as no importation takes place. It follows that if the national economy is to derive the maximum benefit from the impact of international and national tourism, there is an elementary obligation to find all those products needed for tourist consumption. The dynamics of agricultural production in recent years appear to confirm the ability of developing countries to produce the major part of their agricultural products required for tourist consumption without resorting to massive imports. The tourist economy of any country, if it is to remain healthy, must rely upon local agricultural production and this elementary condition seems today to be on the way to realisation in the majority of developing countries.

Tourism Income Multiplier (TIM)

Multipliers are a means of estimating how much extra income is produced in an economy as a result of initial spending or injection of cash. Everytime the money changes hands it provides new income and the continuing series of conversions of money spent by the tourists form the multiplier effect. The more often the conversion occurs, the greater its beneficial effect on the economy of the recipient country.

Infrastructural Development

Development and improvement of infrastructure is another important benefit. The benefits from infrastructure investments, justified primarily for tourism — airports, roads, water supply and other public utilities—may be widely shared by the other sectors of the economy. In addition to development of new infrastructure, the improvements in the existing infrastructure which are undertaken in order to attract tourists is also of crucial importance. These improvements may confer benefits upon the resident population by providing them with amenities which, hitherto, they had enjoyed. Furthermore, the provision of infrastructure may provide the basis or serve as an encouragement for greater economic diversification. A variety of secondary industries may be promoted which may not serve the needs of tourism. Thus, indirectly, tourist expenditure may be responsible for stimulating other economic activities.

One of the characteristics of under development is that of deficiencies in the basic infrastructures, which lie at the root of a series of serious problems related to the development of tourism. Construction of primary infrastructures represents the foundation of any future economic growth, even though they are not directly productive. The tourist industry illustrates the elementary need for basic infrastructures. It has today the important benefit of being able to profit from the existing infrastructures and thus to make a decisive contribution to the growth of the national economy. The traffic arising from international and national tourism, moreover, represents a reward for the capital invested and can now contribute to the financial efforts required for maintenance. The satisfactory degree of development achieved in this specific sector now permits major tourist progress, while giving further proof of the complementary character of tourism in relation to other economic sectors. Creation of basic infrastructures for tourist usage will also be of service to the other sectors of the economy like industry and agriculture. The outcome of this is better equilibrium of general economic growth.

CHAPTER–19

DESTINATION PROMOTION

The Destination Promotion Strategy was carried out by Leithal Thinking to provide a way forward for DEMA. A summary of this strategy is provided below. DEMA will become the central focus for shaping perceptions of Edinburgh across the target areas of visit, invest, live, work and study. It will draw together the consortium of interests in the promotion of the destination and act as the facilitator or hub in leading the messaging about the destination. This document outlines an ambitious marketing strategy designed to enable DEMA to harness a compelling city proposition, and to develop and deliver promotional activity which will lead to a step change in the city's reputation and perception management.

Edinburgh is facing growing competition for visitors, inward investment, students and immigration. Despite its undoubted strengths and famed quality of life, Edinburgh has some weaknesses compared to its city competitors which need to be addressed. Specifically, Edinburgh falls behind on 'pulse' and 'presence', as well as lacking recognition for its contemporary assets. Edinburgh, utilising the Edinburgh Inspiring Capital brand, needs to turn up the volume on its modern, vibrant attributes, balancing these with the key drivers of its historic beauty and unique heritage. It needs to convey compelling stories and examples which build a more surprising and well-rounded impression of what the city has to offer.

At the heart of the strategy is a compelling city proposition and clear audience targeting. The positioning for Edinburgh is rooted in three fundamental brand truths:

1. Historical and architectural beauty
2. Compact in size but rich and diverse in experience
3. A closeness to nature

These truths are encapsulated in the recommended city proposition:

Edinburgh is a world-class capital city, compact but rich in experiences. It combines a contemporary vibrancy with a rich cultural heritage and architectural beauty. And, its closeness to nature gives it a truly elemental feel.

This is in line with the existing Edinburgh Inspiring Capital brand architecture. DEMA is the guardian and champion for the new proposition as well as the custodian of the Edinburgh Inspiring Capital brand.

This proposition has been developed to meet the needs and requirements of the audience for visit, invest, live, work, and study.

Each specific proposition needs to be substantiated with motivating tactical messages supported by credible reasons to believe (RTB's). These, in turn, should be brought to life by memorable and engaging stories and testimonials. DEMA now needs to 'road test' these propositions and messages by conducting qualitative research amongst the target audience.

Tourism and Community Development

Tourism plays an increasingly important role in the development of communities throughout the U.S. Lake States. The benefits of tourism include both tangible (e.g. job creation, state and local tax revenue, etc.) and less tangible (e.g. social structure, quality-of-life, etc.) community effects. In addition, tourism can, and often does, result in less desirable effects on the economic, social, and environmental fabrics of communities. These benefits and costs provide ample opportunity for creative public policy debate.

The University of Wisconsin - Extension (UWEX) has a long and rich history of developing and supporting partnerships throughout the state and the region. Significant tourism educational programs began more than 40 years ago with the work of Professor Isadore Fine and the UW - Madison School of Commerce. Fifteen years later, this initial programming effort was formalized through the formation of the Recreational Resources Center (later named the Tourism Research & Resource Center). This center provided educational programming to assist in community-based tourism planning and applied research. The center was eliminated in 1996 after its budget was reallocated to the Wisconsin Department of Tourism.

Since 1996, many county-based Community, Natural Resource and Economic Development (CNRED) educators have continued to develop and deliver quality tourism programming throughout Wisconsin and beyond. In addition, there continues to be a modest support network of specialists that conduct applied research programs addressing tourism development. Examples of issues addressed in this programming include business development, marketing, outdoor recreation planning, natural resources and amenity-base development, heritage tourism, nature-based tourism, festivals and events, tourism economics, tourism infrastructure, traveler research, and hospitality training. These local, regional, and state-level tourism efforts can greatly benefit from sanction, guidance, support, and packaging in creating an overarching umbrella for CNRED Tourism Programs.

Tourism has been and will continue to be an important component of our social, economic, and environmental heritage. We endeavor to sharing expertise and practices that are transferable to communities in the Lake States and beyond. By doing so, we have an opportunity to establish collaborative networks to help strengthen community-based tourism education and applied research. The literature and web-based resources captured here provide an organizing component intent on fostering this engagement.

This clearinghouse of community tourism resources is created as an evolving resource. We are interested in your suggestions for additions and future directions. Please direct comments to us using the following contact information. We hope you find this useful.

Community Attitudes Towards Tourism Development

In light of empirical evidence indicating the many and varied impacts of tourism to host destinations, various authors (e.g. Andriotis and Vaughan 2003; Lankford and Howard, 1994, p.122) recommended a focus on residents' perceptions of the conditions and changes that may exist in host communities. As has been suggested by some authors (for example, Allen et al., 1988; Andriotis and Vaughan 2003; Lankford & Howard, 1994; Ritchie, 1988) a balance of residents' perceptions of the costs and benefits of tourism is considered a major factor in visitor satisfaction and is, therefore, vital for the success of the tourism industry. Thus, Allen et al. (1988, p. 16) propose that residents perceptions of, and attitudes towards tourism must be continually assessed to ensure that action is taken in good time and through such action the residents are willing partners in the development process. Going forward, awareness of residents' perceptions of tourism development and its impacts can help planners and developers to identify real concerns and issues in order for appropriate policies and action to take place, optimising the benefits and minimising the problems (Andriotis and Vaughan 2003).

Following the significance of community attitudes to the success of a destination, research on community attitudes toward tourists and tourism development has become one of the most systematic and well studied areas in the field of tourism. For instance, Andriotis and Vaughan (2003) have found 83 quantitative published papers in academic journals related to this area of research. Among these community attitudinal studies two frameworks have dominated:

· social exchange theory, that is concerned with "understanding the exchange of resources between individual and groups in an interaction of situation" where "actors supply one another with valued resources" (Ap 1992, p. 668), and

· social representations theory, that is concerned "with describing and understanding how and what people think in their ongoing everyday experiences and how a wider social reality influences these thoughts (Pearce, Moscardo, and Ross, 1996, p. 39)".

On the other hand, the majority of community studies have followed a quantitative approach. Within the extensive quantitative research on community attitudes, the majority applies statistical techniques without actually providing theory. Quantitative methods adopted in attitudinal research can be distinguished according to the statistical techniques they use as follows:

1. Bivariate or single factor approaches that investigate the influence of single factors, such as extrinsic (e.g. degree or stage of the host destination's development, type of tourists and seasonality), and intrinsic (e.g. distance that residents live from tourist zones, economic and/or employment dependency in tourism, length of residency, socio-demographic characteristics),
2. Multivariate or multiple factor approaches, (e.g. factor analysis and cluster analysis), which, unlike

the bivariate, they examine more than one variable simultaneously and

3. The ones that utilise both bivariate and multivariate methods.

Quality Tourism Standards

The Adventure Tourism Council began developing Quality Tourism Standards (QTS) in the early 1990's. Operators' main concerns were based around the need to raise and improve standards in the adventure tourism sector. Several draft codes of practice for various sectors have been developed over the years but until 1999 there had been no consensus on the development of a cost effective, practical solution that resolved administration, branding and marketing issues.

Global Situation—Internationally, quality-based standards are developing across all industry sectors, including tourism. These are typically centred around the international standards organisation series - including the ISO9000 (production) and ISO14000 (environmental) standards. Issues of liability, particularly the right to sue for compensatory and exemplary damages, and the potential effect of the European Travel Directive (European Union clients can sue New Zealand suppliers in their country of origin) are also driving the standards' development.

What are the Quality Tourism Standards?—The aim of QTS is to provide a client-focussed, cost effective, quality standard for providers of tourism products.

Seven different components within the QTS have been identified to date. These are:

1. compliance
2. safety
3. environment
4. cultural

5. service
6. training
7. business
8. facilities.

These are divided into sector-specific and generic components. Sector-specific components (e.g. safety) will be developed by the sectors themselves while generic components (e.g. environmental), will be facilitated by sector groups, TIANZ and other stakeholders.

So Who's Involved?—Below is a sample of the sector specific activities involved.

1. Rafting
2. Jetboating
3. Horse-trekking
4. Sea kayaking
5. All-terrain vehicles
6. Trekking
7. Off-road vehicles
8. Eco/nature tourism
9. Adventure cycling
10. Flight seeing
11. Hunting

All of the above have generic components added to their own sector-specific components.

How Do They Work?—Qualmark will administer and market the QTS programme, and arrange for an annual independent accreditation of the operation. Accreditation will be based on the operator's implementation of the standard and result in the achievment of the Qualmark Visitor Activity Endorsement License. Successfully accredited companies will be able to market themselves as meeting the standard. They'll also be marketed domestically and internationally by

Qualmark and, over time, visitor information centres will give these companies preferential treatment. It's also likely that Tourism New Zealand will make the QTS a minimum qualification for access to their website, international media programme and off-shore marketing.

Responsible Tourism in Destinations

Shaping Sustainable Spaces into Better Places

We, representatives of inbound and outbound tour operators, emerging entrepreneurs in the tourism industry, national parks, provincial conservation authorities, all spheres of government, tourism professionals, tourism authorities, NGOs and hotel groups and other tourism stakeholders, from 20 countries in Africa, North and South America, Europe and Asia; having come together in Cape Town to consider the issue of Responsible Tourism in Destinations have agreed this declaration.

Mindful of the debates at the United Nations Commission on Sustainable Development in 1999, which asserted the importance of the economic, social and environment aspects of sustainable development and of the interests of indigenous peoples and local communities in particular.

Recognising the global challenge of reducing social and economic inequalities and reducing poverty, and the importance of New Partnership for Africa's Development (NEPAD) in the process.

Recognising the importance of the World Tourism Organization's Global Code of Ethics, which aims to promote responsible, sustainable and universally accessible tourism and sharing its commitment to equitable, responsible and sustainable world tourism and its STEP initiative with UNCTAD, which seeks to harness sustainable tourism to help eliminate poverty.

Conscious that we are now ten years on from the Rio Earth Summit on Environment and Development, and that the World Summit on Sustainable Development taking place in Johannesburg will put renewed emphasis on sustainability, economic development, and in particular on poverty reduction.

Aware of the World Tourism Organization, World Travel and Tourism Council and the Earth Council's updated Agenda 21 for the Travel and Tourism Industry and the success achieved by a number of businesses, local communities and national and local governments in moving towards sustainability in tourism.

Aware of the work of the UNEP, and the Tourism Industry Report 2002, and work of UNESCO, and other UN agencies, promoting sustainable tourism in partnership with the private sector, NGOs, civil society organisations and government.

Aware of the guidelines for sustainable tourism in vulnerable ecosystems being developed in the framework of the Convention on Biological Diversity.

Conscious of developments in other industries and sectors, and in particular of the growing international demand for ethical business, and the adoption of clear Corporate Social Responsibility (CSR) policies by companies, and the transparent reporting of achievements in meeting CSR objectives in company annual reports.

Recognising that there has been considerable progress in addressing the environmental impacts of tourism, although there is a long way to go to achieve sustainability; and that more limited progress has been made in harnessing tourism for local economic development, for the benefit of communities and indigenous peoples, and in managing the social impacts of tourism.

Endorsing the Global Code of Ethics and the importance of making all forms of tourism sustainable through all stakeholders taking responsibility for creating better forms of tourism and realising these aspirations.

Relishing the diversity of our world's cultures, habitats and species and the wealth of our cultural and natural heritage, as the very basis of tourism, we accept that responsible and sustainable tourism will be achieved in different ways in different places.

Accepting that, in the words of the Global Code of Ethics, an attitude of tolerance and respect for the diversity of religious, philosophical and moral beliefs, are both the foundation and the consequence of responsible tourism.

Recognising that dialogue, partnerships and multi-stakeholder processes - involving government, business and local communities - to make better places for hosts and guests can only be realised at the local level, and that all stakeholders have different, albeit interdependent, responsibilities; tourism can only be managed for sustainability at the destination level.

Conscious of the importance of good governance and political stability in providing the context for responsible tourism in destinations, and recognising that the devolution of decision making power to democratic local government is necessary to build stable partnerships at a local level, and to the empowerment of local communities.

Aware that the management of tourism requires the participation of a broad range of government agencies and particularly at the local destination level.

Recognising that in order to protect the cultural, social and environmental integrity of destinations limits to tourism development are sometimes necessary.

Having, during the Cape Town Conference, examined the South African Guidelines for Responsible Tourism, tested them in a series of field visits, and explored how tourism can be made to work better for local communities, tourists and businesses alike, we recognise their value in helping to shape sustainable tourism in South Africa.

Recognising that one of the strengths of the South African Guidelines for Responsible Tourism is that they were developed through a national consultative process, and that they reflect the priorities and aspirations of the South African people.

Recognising that Responsible Tourism takes many forms, that different destinations and stakeholders will have different priorities, and that local policies and guidelines will need to be developed through multi-stakeholder processes to develop responsible tourism in destinations.

Having the following characteristics, Responsible Tourism:

1. Minimises negative economic, environmental, and social impacts;
2. Generates greater economic benefits for local people and enhances the well-being of host communities, improves working conditions and access to the industry;
3. Involves local people in decisions that affect their lives and life chances;
4. Makes positive contributions to the conservation of natural and cultural heritage, to the maintenance of the world's diversity;
5. Provides more enjoyable experiences for tourists through more meaningful connections with local people, and a greater understanding of local cultural, social and environmental issues;
6. Provides access for physically challenged people; and
7. Is culturally sensitive, engenders respect between tourists and hosts, and builds local pride and confidence

We call upon countries, multilateral agencies, destinations and enterprises to develop similar practical guidelines and to encourage planning authorities, tourism businesses, tourists and local communities - to take responsibility for achieving sustainable tourism, and to create better places for people to live in and for people to visit.

We urge multilateral agencies responsible for development strategies to include sustainable responsible tourism in their outcomes.

Determined to make tourism more sustainable, and accepting that it is the responsibility of all stakeholders in tourism to achieve more sustainable forms of tourism, we commit ourselves to pursue the principles of Responsible Tourism.

Convinced that it is primarily in the destinations, the places that tourists visit, where tourism enterprises conduct their business and where local communities and tourists and the tourism industry interact, that the economic, social and environmental impacts of tourism need to be managed responsibly, to maximise positive impacts and minimise negative ones.

We undertake to work in concrete ways in destinations to achieve better forms of tourism and to work with other stakeholders in destinations. We commit to build the capacity of all stakeholders in order to ensure that they can secure an effective voice in decision making. We uphold the guiding principles for Responsible Tourism which were identified:

Guiding Principles for Economic Responsibility

1. Assess economic impacts before developing tourism and exercise preference for those forms of development that benefit local communities and minimise negative impacts on local livelihoods (for example through loss of access to resources), recognising that tourism may not always be the most appropriate form of local economic development
2. Maximise local economic benefits by increasing linkages and reducing leakages, by ensuring that

communities are involved in, and benefit from, tourism. Wherever possible use tourism to assist in poverty reduction by adopting pro-poor strategies

3. Develop quality products that reflect, complement, and enhance the destination
4. Market tourism in ways which reflect the natural, cultural and social integrity of the destination, and which encourage appropriate forms of tourism
5. Adopt equitable business practises, pay and charge fair prices, and build partnerships in ways in which risk is minimised and shared, and recruit and employ staff recognising international labour standards
6. Provide appropriate and sufficient support to small, medium and micro enterprises to ensure tourism-related enterprises thrive and are sustainable

Guiding Principles for Social Responsibility

1. Actively involve the local community in planning and decision-making and provide capacity building to make this a reality
2. Assess social impacts throughout the life cycle of the operation - including the planning and design phases of projects - in order to minimise negative impacts and maximise positive ones
3. Endeavour to make tourism an inclusive social experience and to ensure that there is access for all, in particular vulnerable and disadvantaged communities and individuals
4. Combat the sexual exploitation of human beings, particularly the exploitation of children
5. Be sensitive to the host culture, maintaining and encouraging social and cultural diversity
6. Endeavour to ensure that tourism contributes to improvements in health and education

Guiding Principles for Environmental Responsibility

1. Assess environmental impacts throughout the life cycle of tourist establishments and operations – including the planning and design phase - and ensure that negative impacts are reduced to the minimum and maximising positive ones
2. Use resources sustainably, and reduce waste and over-consumption
3. Manage natural diversity sustainably, and where appropriate restore it; and consider the volume and type of tourism that the environment can support, and respect the integrity of vulnerable ecosystems and protected areas
4. Promote education and awareness for sustainable development – for all stakeholders
5. Raise the capacity of all stakeholders and ensure that best practice is followed, for this purpose consult with environmental and conservation experts

We recognise that this list is not exhaustive and that multi-stakeholder groups in diverse destinations should adapt these principles to reflect their own culture and environment.

Responsible tourism seeks to maximise positive impacts and to minimise negative ones. Compliance with all relevant international and national standards, laws and regulations is assumed. Responsibility, and the market advantage that can go with it, is about doing more than the minimum.

We recognise that the transparent and auditable reporting of progress towards achieving responsible tourism targets and benchmarking, is essential to the integrity and credibility of our work, to the ability of all stakeholders to assess progress, and to enable consumers to exercise effective choice.

We commit to making our contribution to move towards a more balanced relationship between hosts and guests in destinations, and to create better places for local communities and indigenous peoples; and recognising that this can only be achieved by government, local communities and business cooperating on practical initiatives in destinations.

We call upon tourism enterprises and trade associations in originating markets and in destinations to adopt a responsible approach, to commit to specific responsible practises, and to report progress in a transparent and auditable way, and where appropriate to use this for market advantage. Corporate businesses can assist by providing markets, capacity building, mentoring and micro-financing support for small, medium and micro enterprises.

In order to implement the guiding principles for economic, social and environmental responsibility, it is necessary to use a portfolio of tools, which will include regulations, incentives, and multi-stakeholder participatory strategies. Changes in the market encouraged by consumer campaigns and new marketing initiatives also contribute to market driven change.

Local authorities have a central role to play in achieving responsible tourism through commitment to supportive policy frameworks and adequate funding. We call upon local authorities and tourism administrations to develop - through multi-stakeholder processes - destination management strategies and responsible tourism guidelines to create better places for host communities and the tourists who visit. Local Agenda 21 programs, with their participatory and monitoring processes, are particularly useful.

We call upon the media to exercise responsibility in the way in which they portray tourism destinations, to avoid raising false expectations and to provide balanced and fair reporting. We all have a responsibility to make a difference by the way we act.

BIBLIOGRAPHY

- "AJ Hackett Bungy". Bungy.co.nz. AJHackettBungy. Bungy.co.nz.
- Barzilai, Gad. 2003. Communities and Law: Politics and Cultures of Legal Identities. Ann Arbor: University of Michigan Press.
- Chavis, D.M., Hogge, J.H., McMillan, D.W., & Wandersman, A. 1986. "Sense of community through Brunswick's lens: A first look." Journal of Community Psychology, 14(1), 24-40.
- Chipuer, H. M., & Pretty, G. M. H. (1999). A review of the Sense of Community Index: Current uses, factor structure, reliability, and further development. Journal of Community Psychology, 27(6), 643-658.
- Cymerman, A; Rock, PB. Medical Problems in High Mountain Environments. A Handbook for Medical Officers. USARIEM-TN94-2. US Army Research Inst. of Environmental Medicine Thermal and Mountain Medicine Division Technical Report.
- Durkheim, Émile. 1950 [1895] The Rules of Sociological Method. Translated by S. A. Solovay and J. H. Mueller. New York: The Free Press.
- Eric Larson, 2003 p135, The Devil in the White City; Murder, Magic, and Madness at the Fair that Changed America. Citing Chicago Tribune, Nov. 9, 1889.

• McMillan, D.W., & Chavis, D.M. 1986. "Sense of community: A definition and theory." American Journal of Community Psychology, 14(1), 6-23.

• Mike Barber needed to fly 1% further than Ruhmer's 435 miles (700 km) in order to break the official FAI record; Barber needed to fly only 3 more miles for a total of 440 miles (710 km). Barber's flight remains the longest hang glider flight ever.

• Mountainous plateau creates ozone "halo" around Tibet

• Muza, SR; Fulco, CS; Cymerman, A (2004). "Altitude Acclimatization Guide.". US Army Research Inst. of Environmental Medicine Thermal and Mountain Medicine Division Technical Report (USARIEM-TN-04-05).

• Nancy, Jean-Luc. La Communauté désœuvrée - philosophical questioning of the concept of community and the possibility of encountering a non-subjective concept of it

• Newman, D. 2005. Sociology: Exploring the Architecture of Everyday Life, Chapter 5. "Building Identity: Socialization" Pine Forge Press. Retrieved: 2006-08-05.

• Peck, M.S. 1987. The Different Drum: Community-Making and Peace. New York: Simon and Schuster. ISBN 0-684-84858-9

• Perkins, D.D., Florin, P., Rich, R.C., Wandersman, A. & Chavis, D.M. (1990). Participation and the social and physical environment of residential blocks: Crime and community context. American Journal of Community Psychology, 18, 83-115.

• Putnam, R. D. 2000. Bowling Alone: The collapse and revival of American community. New York: Simon and Schuster

• Sarason, S.B. 1974. The psychological sense of community: Prospects for a community psychology. San Francisco: Jossey-Bass.

INDEX